*“With biblical insight,*
*and James coach us pas*
*as we negotiate the m*
*the deep wisdom of these pages and commend this book to every fellow pastor.”*

**Dane Ortlund**, Author, *Gentle and Lowly*
Senior Pastor, Naperville Presbyterian Church

*“Croft and Carroll have provided a very important text for those either in church leadership or aspiring toward it. With biblical depth and practical wisdom, they lay out a model for developing pastors and carrying out the ministry with a Word-centered, theologically driven methodology. This kind of principled leadership will always run longer, better, and farther than personality-driven pragmatism. Pastoral perseverance is a great need today, and I pray that this book will help toward this end.”*

**Tony Merida**, Author, *Love Your Church*
Pastor, Imago Dei Church, Raleigh, NC

*“How do pastors break the trend of short pastorates and short ministries? It takes pastoral perseverance to continue through the rigors of ministry. Brian Croft and James Carroll in* Pastoral Perseverance: Helping pastors stay, endure, and thrive *provide a well-thought-out roadmap toward pastoral perseverance. Avoiding cliche-type advice, they face the barriers to perseverance with biblical answers applied in the crucible of real-life ministry. I finished the book encouraged and refreshed, with new insight to press on in ministry. Pastors, read this book to put wind in your pastoral sails. Church members, read this book to know how to better serve your pastors.”*

**Phil A. Newton**, PhD, Retired pastor
Author, *40 Questions About Pastoral Ministry*
Director of Pastoral Care & Mentoring for the Pillar Network

*"If you're called to ministry, be careful. You're in for a rough go of it mentally, physically, and spiritually. It's always tempting to unplug, either by throwing in the towel and quitting or by becoming a robot just going through the motions. Brian Croft and James Carroll argue there's a better way – the path of Jesus, the faithful shepherd who didn't run away and flee when he saw the wolf coming. Stick with Jesus and his word, counsel brothers Croft and Carroll. Their book is no glib cliché-ridden formula for success, but the transparent record of their own mistakes and failures transformed by the faithfulness of a very gracious God who always keeps his promises."*

**Harold L. Senkbeil**
Author, *The Care of Souls*

*"As disinterest towards the church increases, pastors will be pressed to find wise guidance and godly motivation for shepherding. Well acquainted with the challenges of ministry, Croft and Carroll offer a biblical, systematic, and wise treatment of pastoral perseverance. But they also address the heart, urging pastors not only to preach the gospel of grace but to imbibe in it. Here is a needed guide for pastors in our times."*

**Jonathan Dodson**
Author, *The Unwavering Pastor*
Founder of gcdiscipleship.com

# PASTORAL **PERSEVERANCE**

## HELPING PASTORS STAY, ENDURE, AND THRIVE

BRIAN CROFT
& JAMES CARROLL

Scripture quotations are from The Holy Bible, English Standard Version, ESV®. Text Edition: 2016. Copyright © 2001 by Crossway Bibles, a publishing ministry of Good News Publishers.

Copyright © 2023 by Brian Croft and James Carroll

First published in Great Britain in 2023

The right of Brian Croft and James Carroll to be identified as the Authors of this Work has been asserted by them in accordance with the Copyright, Designs and Patents Act 1988.

All rights reserved. No part of this publication may be reproduced, stored in a retrieval system or transmitted in any form or by any means, electronic, mechanical, photocopying, recording or otherwise, without the prior permission of the publisher or the Copyright Licensing Agency.

British Library Cataloguing in Publication Data
A record for this book is available from the British Library

ISBN: 978-1-783973-54-5

Designed and typeset by Pete Barnsley (CreativeHoot.com)

Printed in UK

Evangelical Press, an imprint of 10Publishing
Unit C, Tomlinson Road, Leyland, PR25 2DY, England

email: epbooks@10ofthose.com
website: 10ofThose.com

1 3 5 7 10 8 6 4 2

# CONTENTS

Introduction ........ 1

A Need to Qualify ........ 7

A Call to Take Heed ........ 25

A Conviction to Shepherd ........ 45

An Urgency to Preach ........ 65

A Tenacity to Suffer ........ 83

A Resolve to Die ........ 101

Conclusion ........ 117

# INTRODUCTION

We are nearing the precipice of a crisis. If pastors continue leaving the ministry in droves as they are, the church will face a vacuum of leadership in the next generation. Recent statistics reveal that 50% of current pastors in America will exit the ministry in five years, and a staggering 80% will depart in ten years.[1] But we might not be waiting that long for a watershed as 42% of pastors considered quitting in 2022.[2] These statistics reveal one of the primary factors contributing to the closure of approximately 5,000 churches in the U.S. each year. Once again, evangelicals could well be heading toward a climactic moment as pastors resign en masse and sheep are left wandering. While observers and commentators speculate as to why these trends exist, supposed experts present a wide variety of solutions for reversing them. The tragedy is that many of these so-called "solutions" only serve to compound the problem because they sidestep the heart of the real issue while inadvertently contributing to it. Consider two examples.

The first of these is pragmatism, which seems to have been the most popular answer to any church problem in the last 100 years. This response surely predates the twentieth century, but the record of its proliferation in recent years is stunning. Pragmatism is a philosophical theory that determines value and

1 Research done by Soul Shepherd Institute.

2 "Pastors Share Top Reasons They've Considered Quitting Ministry in the Past Year" (Barna Group, April 27, 2022); https://www.barna.com/research/pastors-quitting-ministry/ (accessed January 31, 2023).

truth by observing what works or by what achieves a particular end. More than mere pragmatic thinking that pursues efficiency and effectiveness, this ideology is beholden to outcomes regardless of the cost or sacrifices involved in achieving them. As such, it rejects the notion that the Bible is sufficient for informing and guiding us on how to live faithfully in the world. While proponents of pragmatism in the church will almost always acknowledge the Bible as *a* source of truth, they will refuse to accept it as the primary or sufficient one in matters of practice. Instead, a pragmatist holds that objective reality is found on the basis of observable results. Whatever works must be right or true. Theology, or what we believe about God, necessarily takes a back seat to successful methodology.

Living this way can be dangerous in many aspects of life because it's so easy to confuse correlation and causation. Starvation diets avoid obesity and produce smaller physical bodies, but they fail to promote long-term health and ultimately will lead to death. Even worse, adopting this approach with regard to spiritual matters is eternally destructive, both to individuals and to a church. Pragmatism will inevitably lead Christians to pursue shortcuts in their spiritual progress, such as a legalistic religion in place of heart transformation through spiritual discipline. Likewise, pastors and church leaders who hold this commitment will employ growth strategies and techniques from secular organizations to yield faster results or to meet superficial goals like numeric increase. Biblical exhortations for faithful ministry are replaced by faddish, cultural trends as the foundation for building the church. The driving force becomes what will produce measurable outcomes. As you can imagine, the product is a church established on entertainment, consumerism, and flashy programs with spiritually shallow members. The pastors and church leaders often achieve their goal of attracting bigger crowds and more members to the detriment of everyone's spiritual well-being, including their own. The façade will crumble, leaving despondent pastors struggling in its wake.

A second response to the growing problem comes in the form of personality-driven pastoral leadership. Of course, spiritual, servant leadership is a necessary function in any organization, and a biblically required aspect of a local church. However, this approach stretches the concept of leadership to a grossly unhelpful level by prizing the leader himself over and against his ministry of the word and his faithful care of souls. Feeding off the leader's magnetism, this solution relies on a winsome and clever persona instead of valuing Christ-like character qualities like humility, integrity, and godliness. Rather than requiring the leader to spend his time and talent to fulfill a self-sacrificing, Christ-honoring ministry in shepherding God's people, this paradigm elevates the leader above the people, making him the epicenter and main attraction. Consequently, this approach creates a CEO, top-down structure of leadership that relies too heavily on one person and de-emphasizes the power of God in the gospel through a biblical model of shared ministry.

Capable leaders may shoulder the burden well for a time, and the church may even enjoy a thriving season of numeric growth. However, the bubble will inevitably burst. Unfortunately, many times the leader collapses in burnout under the weight of expectations and pressure, or he spirals into sin leading to disqualification because his charisma outpaces his character. Other times the church implodes from controversy because of a lack of broad, stable leadership. Regardless of the specific brand of dysfunction that characterizes the downfall, this approach is untenable at best and ungodly at worst. Even when the church experiences apparent success, glory is given to the human leader instead of God.

The net result, then, of either pragmatism or of the elevation of leadership personalities is a church that is weaker than it appears and a pastor who is simultaneously weighed down and propped up by worldly expectations. While they may defy our original statistics in the short term, they are destined to contribute to them in the long term.

The harm from implementing these destructive strategies extends well beyond the churches that formally embrace them. These techniques crush the soul of the average pastor who ministers in the shadow of the false expectations such approaches produce. Ordinary pastors labor in the trenches, rightly trusting in the Lord's timing and fighting to keep their eye on the goal of faithfulness instead of numeric growth. Unfortunately, the awareness of these seemingly successful models, and others like them, can tempt pastors away from contentment in serving God and shepherding souls toward the more glamorous role of business-like CEO. Others will fall into sinful self-pity and despondency as they watch enviously as others "succeed" while they struggle to gain traction in helping others make true spiritual progress. While these pastors are culpable for their sinful responses, we must acknowledge the tempting environment created by these so-called "solutions." In addition, these toxic tendencies combine with most pastors' general lack of knowledge and training in self-care to yield a burn-out rate represented in the aforementioned stats. As a result, pastoral perseverance becomes an unobtainable reality for most, regardless of the effort, education, and commitment of a pastor.

Nevertheless, hope is not lost! God desires that pastors persevere in their assigned ministry fields, and he has provided the necessary resources to make it happen. This biblical principle does not mean every pastor will serve only one flock or at only one ministry post, as God providentially guides each one according to his eternal purposes. We can, however, reasonably conclude from specific biblical texts that staying, enduring, and thriving over the long-haul ought to be the rule and not the exception. The growing tide of pastors burning out or abandoning their ministry calls into question how many are truly fulfilling their God-appointed mission and finishing their race well.

Thankfully, God not only desires pastoral perseverance, but has planned and provided for it. By God's grace we can seek to build healthy, vibrant churches that rely on the Spirit as pastors are freed to "preach the word . . . in season and out of season" (2 Tim. 4:2). Church members can be well cared for both physically and spiritually as pastors are encouraged to "shepherd the flock . . . among you" (1 Pet. 5:2), grounded in the conviction that pastors will "give an account" to Jesus for every soul under their care (Heb. 13:17; 1 Pet. 5:1–4). This timeless solution results in a local church still led well and organized efficiently without the pastor losing sight of his calling to take heed to himself (Acts 20:28), to be a servant like Jesus (Mark 10:43–45), and to be an example of that service to his flock (1 Pet. 5:3).

In search of God's plan for every pastor that leads to his and the church's thriving, we move away from the lure of these popular modern strategies and to the Scripture. This approach will equip a man who has been saved by the blood of Christ and called to this noble calling of pastoring God's flock. He will be prepared for longevity regardless of his gifting, personality, or education. All this will be through the power of the Holy Spirit for the glory of God, the blessing of God's people, and the building of God's church.

This book explores that divine plan and how it applies to every pastor who desires to persevere and finish well in his work. We will argue that he must embrace six core principles:

A need to qualify
A call to take heed
A conviction to shepherd
An urgency to preach
A tenacity to suffer
A resolve to die

These six areas draw upon some of the most significant passages in the New Testament related to pastoral ministry. They show how this biblical teaching shapes the call, conviction, and role of those appointed by the Chief Shepherd to care for his people. We will consider the basic meaning and thrust of each passage, interact with its ongoing significance, and share our own testimonies—both the good and the bad—related to it.

These passages paint a true and sober portrait of this grueling and joyful work rather than the glamorous one imagined by so many in our day. As Bonhoeffer famously wrote, "When Christ calls a man, He bids him come and die."[3] Thus, we are not surprised to find that God's plan for his under-shepherds is one of suffering, sacrifice, and service to others that often bears more eternal than temporal fruit. Yet for those divinely called by God to this pastoral work, it stirs the soul bringing joy and purpose unlike anything else in this world. We are praying that God will allow this book to bring you a proper understanding of this plan and to use it to set your expectations and prepare you for what is coming—so that he will ultimately empower you by his Spirit to persevere.

---

3 Dietrich Bonhoeffer, The Cost of Discipleship (New York: Macmillan, 1963), p. 99.

# 1

# A NEED TO QUALIFY

*The saying is trustworthy: If anyone aspires to the office of overseer, he desires a noble task.*
(1 Tim. 3:1)

A great need emerged early in my (Brian) pastoral ministry. The church I was serving saw steady growth in the first few years, including attracting several students from a local seminary. As I built relationships with these young men pursuing pastoral ministry, I found they had many wonderful qualities. Each one of them was genuinely devoted to God, had been transformed by the gospel, loved the local church, and sensed God's leading to pursue full-time vocational ministry. As a result, each one had come to seminary with the expectation that they would be trained and equipped for this important work with eternal impact.

As I grew to know these young men, however, I was concerned by some common elements in their stories. Most had come to the seminary without any kind of congregational affirmation from a local church. Despite the seminary requiring this for admission, I learned after some investigation that, in most cases, their church's affirmation amounted to little more than a letter of approval for them to attend the school. None had experienced a corporate affirmation of their gifts for the ministry, and none had been tested or trained by the leadership and congregation in their respective church. They had permission to attend, but not the affirmation and support from the local body of believers as a man gifted and called by God to shepherd and lead his people.

I also discovered these students—in most cases reflecting the view of their respective home churches—expected the seminary would fulfill this role by affirming and preparing them for the duties, challenges, and struggles of ministry. But as Albert Mohler, president of the Southern Baptist Theological Seminary, has stated on more than one occasion, this is not the role or responsibility of a seminary:

> *I emphatically believe that the best and most proper place for the education and preparation of pastors is in the local church. We should be ashamed that churches fail miserably in their responsibility to train future pastors. Established pastors should be ashamed if they are not pouring themselves into the lives of young men whom God has called into the teaching and leadership ministry of the church.*[1]

In other words, seminaries do not and should not shoulder the responsibility for selecting, testing, and affirming men for ministerial calling. Instead, this task falls under the authority of the local church, who is ultimately accountable to God for it. Their failure to do so has placed unnecessary pressure on seminaries and Bible colleges, led to widespread confusion among men seeking a pastoral calling for ministry, and fostered a neglect in the local church of a divine mandate to prepare the next generation of shepherds for God's flock.

Charles Bridges (1794–1869) has provided arguably the best work on the responsibility and the process of assessing men for ministry. In his seminal book *The Christian Ministry*, Bridges

1 Quoted in Adrian Warnock's blog post, "Interview with Dr. Albert Mohler" (November 8, 2006); http://adrianwarnock.com/2006/11/interview-dr-albert-mohler-radio-host.htm (accessed October 15, 2013).

places the responsibility for the determination of one's call on both the conscience of the individual and the local church to which he is committed. Bridges refers to these two aspects of calling as the internal and the external call of God:

> *The external call is a commission received from and recognized by the Church . . . not indeed qualifying the Minister, but accrediting him, whom God had internally and suitably qualified. This call communicates therefore only official authority. The internal call is the voice and power of the Holy Ghost, directing the will and the judgment, and conveying personal qualifications. Both calls, however—though essentially distinct in their character and source—are indispensable for the exercise of our commission.*[2]

Bridges argues that an individual must receive inward leading from God to know he is truly set aside by him to serve in the ministry. This inner sense is recognized through a God-given desire to do ministry combined with a conviction that he has been gifted and empowered by God's Spirit for this work. In addition to, and consistent with the internal call, an individual must possess an external call. This is the vital affirmation from a local church that he does indeed possess the gifts and godly character suitable for a Christian minister. Many other godly men throughout church history have agreed that both the internal and external calls are necessary for a man to serve in pastoral ministry.

A local church, then, ought to think biblically before acting to endorse a man's pursuit of ministry. Sadly, many churches today base their affirmation on nothing more than a given man's sense of *internal calling*—that is, his subjective, and unfalsifiable, perception of a desire and giftedness to do the work—or on

---

2 Charles Bridges, The Christian Ministry: An Inquiry into the Causes of Its Inefficiency (Edinburgh: Banner of Truth, 1967), pp. 91–92.

his charisma and the outward appearance of gifting. However, churches must instead base their approval primarily on an objective and tangible process that tests his character and gifting for ministry according to Scripture.

That leaves us to ponder the question: "What kind of man receives an external call from a local church?" The aim of this chapter is to consider, with the help of wisdom from pastors and theologians throughout church history, how the biblical qualifications for pastoral ministry should be employed to evaluate men sensing an internal calling from God. Answers are offered in light of the biblical qualifications for pastors found in 1 Timothy 3:1–7:

> *The saying is trustworthy: If anyone aspires to the office of overseer, he desires a noble task. Therefore an overseer must be above reproach, the husband of one wife, sober-minded, self-controlled, respectable, hospitable, able to teach, not a drunkard, not violent but gentle, not quarrelsome, not a lover of money. He must manage his own household well, with all dignity keeping his children submissive, for if someone does not know how to manage his own household, how will he care for God's church? He must not be a recent convert, or he may become puffed up with conceit and fall into the condemnation of the devil. Moreover, he must be well thought of by outsiders, so that he may not fall into disgrace, into a snare of the devil.*

This well-known passage establishes the need for pastors to demonstrate that they are qualified for the work of shepherding God's flock.[3] We will summarize the necessary qualities that show a man's fitness for ministry into four broad categories.

3 Tit. 1:6–9 and 1 Pet. 5:1–4 are also clear, complimentary passages describing these biblical qualifications

## TRANSFORMED BY THE GOSPEL

While it should be entirely obvious, we find it important to state outright that no man is qualified to enter the sacred office of being a minister of the gospel unless he has himself been transformed by the gospel. The gospel is the message of God's plan and work to save sinners from his wrath and reconcile them to himself through the person and work of Jesus Christ—his life, death, resurrection, and ascension—and the offer of that salvation is to all who will turn from sin and trust fully in Jesus. A sinner receives this salvation as a gift of God's grace through repentance of sin and personal faith in Jesus. While it seems bizarre for a man to give his life to preaching the gospel and serving God's church without first experiencing the saving work of Christ, it is a legitimate concern. Hence, in the seventeenth century, Richard Baxter began his celebrated book, *The Reformed Pastor*, in this way:

> *Take heed to yourselves, lest you be void of that saving grace of God which you offer to others, and be strangers to the effectual working of that gospel which you preach; and lest, while you proclaim to the world the necessity of a Saviour, your own hearts should neglect him and you should miss of an interest in him and his saving benefits. Take heed to yourselves, lest you perish, while you call upon others to take heed of perishing; and lest you famish yourselves while you prepare food for them. . . . Many have warned others that they come not to that place of torment, while yet they hastened to it themselves; many a preacher is now in hell, who hath a hundred times called upon his hearers to use the utmost care and diligence to escape it.*[4]

4 Richard Baxter, The Reformed Pastor, ed. William Brown (Edinburgh: Banner of Truth, 2001), p. 53.

Baxter's warning should resonate with those of us who love Christ and his church just as much in the twenty-first century. When local churches fail to discern whether a man is still in darkness, enslaved to sin, and in complete rebellion against God before placing him in a pastoral position, they place God's people in a dangerous position. If the man is perishing, how can he properly warn other sinners or shepherd saints?

This qualification simply cannot be assumed. If a man has not been transformed by Christ, he is not fit for pastoral ministry.

## DESIRE FOR THE WORK

The Apostle Paul instructs Timothy, his young protégé in the faith, by writing, "The saying is trustworthy: If anyone aspires to the office of overseer [pastor], he desires a noble task" (1 Tim. 3:1). The great nineteenth-century Baptist, Charles Spurgeon, lectured young men preparing for the ministry in this way, "The first sign of the heavenly calling is an intense, all-absorbing desire for the work."[5] There must be a strong, unquenchable desire to do the work of a pastor—a desire to preach God's word, shepherd God's people, evangelize the lost, disciple the spiritually immature, and serve the local church.

Spurgeon continues that this divine aspiration becomes evident through an urgency to do nothing else:

> *If any student in this room could be content to be a newspaper editor, or a grocer, or a farmer, or a doctor, or a lawyer, or a senator, or a king, in the name of heaven and earth, let him go his way; he is not the man in whom dwells the Spirit of God in its fullness, for a man so filled with God would utterly weary of any pursuit but that for which his inmost soul pants.*

5 C.H. Spurgeon, Lectures to My Students (Grand Rapids, MI: Zondervan Publishing House, 1954), p. 26.

*If on the other hand, you can say that for all the wealth of both the Indies you could not and dare not espouse any other calling so as to be put aside from preaching the gospel of Jesus Christ, then depend upon it, if other things be equally satisfactory, you have the signs of this apostleship. We must feel that woe is unto us if we preach not the gospel; the word of God must be unto us as fire in our bones, otherwise, if we undertake the ministry, we shall be unhappy in it, shall be unable to bear the self-denials incident to it, and shall be of little service to those among whom we minister.*[6]

Yet, because this work is noble or good, it may attract men whose desire for it is driven by a longing to be respected. Therefore, churches must investigate carefully to discern that the unquenchable yearning is for the work and not merely temporal return. This distinction is important because the work is fraught with struggles, challenges, discouragements, pressures, and spiritual battles that can cripple the strongest of men. If the desire for this divine labor is weak, ordinary, or self-serving, it will slip when your brother betrays you, weaken when your job is threatened, or fade when physical, mental, and emotional fatigue set in. This aspiration must so define the individual that the reality of an internal calling is unmistakable. Its strength, which results from the Spirit's enabling and equipping work in us, empowers pastoral perseverance. Basil Manly, Jr. captures not just the desire of the internal calling, but how that desire should increase over time:

*This steadfast and divinely implanted desire to labor for souls is substantially what is meant by "the internal call." It may be*

6 Spurgeon, Lectures to My Students, pp. 26–27.

> *distinguished from the early zeal, which young converts usually have, and which generally subsides into a calm principle of benevolent activity in their own particular sphere. In the man truly called, it grows, it increases. As he reflects on it, and prays about it, the great salvation becomes greater and nearer to him than when he first believed; the guilt and ruin of immortal souls weigh heavily upon him; he feels impelled to warn them to flee the wrath to come. Sometimes the thought presses on one, so that he cannot rest. The strongest promptings of self-interest, the greatest timidity and natural reserve, the most violent opposition of irreligious relatives and influential friends, and even the most serious peril, prove insufficient to check this holy ardor. The man is made to feel that for him all other avocations are trifling, all worldly employments unattractive. "Woe is unto me," he cries, "if I preach not the gospel!" Jails, and fetters, and the stake, have no terrors for him comparable with the guilt of disobeying Jesus, and the frown of his redeemer.*[7]

Only a man who is fully trusting in Jesus for salvation and possessing this "irresistible, overwhelming craving and raging thirst"[8] for the work of shepherding God's people should receive a church's affirmation, or external call, to it.

## GODLY CHARACTER AND LIFE

Many faithful, godly men throughout the ages, who displayed Christ in their character and modeled sacrificial service to his church, were not called to the work of pastor/elder. Paul provides Timothy—and thus local churches—with a distinct list of qualifications for any who would serve the church in

7 Michael A.G. Haykin, Roger D. Duke, and A. James Fuller, Soldiers of Christ: Selections from the Writings of Basil Manly, Sr. and Basil Manly, Jr. (Cape Coral, FL: Founders Press, 2009), pp. 175–176.

8 Spurgeon, Lectures to My Students, p. 26.

office of pastor/elder. This list, though similar in many regards to the qualifications for those serving as deacons (1 Tim. 3:8–13), demonstrates the uniqueness of the calling and work of a pastor. It also provides the criteria for evaluating externally and objectively a man who expresses a desire for this work. Fifteen qualifications are given for the office of the pastor, but these can be summarized into five categories:

**Able to teach**

This qualification sets apart the work of a pastor from all others in the church, including those who serve as deacons. Paul identifies this characteristic with a single word, διδακτικόν, which is translated as "apt or able to teach" (1 Tim. 3:2). This adjective refers not just to a man's desire to teach, but to him having the skill and ability to explain and apply God's word faithfully, accurately, and effectively. Paul further confirms the importance of this prerequisite elsewhere by exhorting Timothy, "By the Holy Spirit who dwells within us, guard the good deposit" of the gospel, which God has entrusted to pastors and teachers (2 Tim. 1:14).

The warning of stricter judgment for those who teach in the church, which is found in James 3:1, also emphasizes the gravity of this requirement. Even for those men who are gifted by God for this task, they must exercise these gifts humbly, clearly, passionately, and faithfully. It's not merely what a man can do that matters, but that he employ his gifts in God-honoring ways. Paul charges Timothy to preach the word whatever the cost, seizing every opportunity to make the gospel clear, presenting the treasure and value of Christ before their hearers, and calling all people to repent and believe. The same command falls to us as we trust in the power of the Holy Spirit to perform the transforming work of the gospel. This ability to wield God's word by instructing patiently as a means to "reprove, rebuke, and exhort" (2 Tim. 4:2) defines faithful gospel ministry, both public and private. As Roger Ellsworth has rightly observed, "Fail here and you would have failed in your central task."[9]

**A blameless reputation**

Moving beyond the ministry of teaching, the pastor "must be above reproach" (1 Tim. 3:2). This quality emphasizes that pastors do not merely flee from evil, but even from the appearance of it. As such, this type of man lives above accusations through the consistency of his godly life and reputation among all people. His self-control (which is evident in his not being in bondage to any substance), his gentleness, and his commitment to making peace form the ground of other people's perspective of him.

This blamelessness is certainly not perfection, but a consistent striving for godliness that shapes a pastor's reputation among those who are outside the church. In addition to strengthening his ministry, awareness of the importance of his broader standing in the community serves to protect him from sin and the devil's snare (1 Tim. 3:7). This command is by no means a call to appease the world, but to live reputably so the lost may observe our good deeds and "glorify God on the day of visitation" (1 Pet. 2:12).

**Faithfully manage his family**

Paul states flatly and famously that a pastor must be "the husband of one wife" in both 1 Timothy 3:2 and in Titus 1:6. This phrase is commonly misunderstood to refer only to marriage status, and thus wrongly requiring marriage for pastors and eliminating single men from serving. This qualification, however, demands fidelity based on the presumption that

9 Thomas K. Ascol, ed., Dear Timothy: Letters on Pastoral Ministry (Cape Coral, FL: Founders Press, 2004), p. 272.

most pastors would be married. Using Paul's admonition to all husbands in Ephesians 5:25, pastors ought to love their wives "as Christ loved the church and gave himself up for her." In leading his wife, therefore, the pastor displays genuine and sacrificial love and so provides a model for other men. The command applies to unmarried pastors as well. However, their fidelity takes the form of celibacy and is manifested in Christ-honoring relationships with women.

This charge of faithfulness also applies to the pastor's relationship to—and leadership of—the children in his home. He must shepherd, teach, care for, and manage his children faithfully (1 Tim. 3:4). Once again, this admonition does not require that he have children or that they be converted, but that they respect his authority as the God-appointed head and leader of the family. The exercise of his headship in the home is important for demonstrating the quality of his leadership because "if someone does not know how to manage his own household, how will he care for God's church?" (1 Tim. 3:5).

Another characteristic related to a man's leadership of his family emerges from their hospitality. Many readers associate this characteristic exclusively with welcoming people in the home, which is certainly part of it. However, it also implies welcoming and loving strangers. This element is critical for emphasizing the distinction between people who extend hospitality only to those they know and love, and people who extend it to strangers as well. Pastors must model this sacrificial willingness to care for others, and they should lead their households to embrace this role as the calling for the entire family.

### Godly character

In one regard, all the descriptions from Paul's list could be lumped into this broad category of godly character. For example, the pastor must be "sober-minded, self-controlled, respectable" (1 Tim. 3:2), as well as "gentle, not quarrelsome" (1 Tim. 3:3). These speak of the inward transformation of the gospel reflected outwardly in kindness, compassion, self-control in word and deed, honorableness, humility, discernment, and wisdom. It's impossible to overstate this requirement, as Basil Manly, Jr. observed:

> *It need scarcely be said that piety is essential. No amount of talent, no extent of education, no apparent brilliancy of fervor, should even be allowed to gain admission into the ministry for one whose piety there is a reason to doubt, or who has not a more than ordinary active and consistent holiness. A Christless minister is as horribly out of place as a ghastly skeleton in the pulpit bearing a torch in his hand.*[10]

Ministers must not merely possess these godly characteristics, but they must also daily grow in them, as David Dickson writes:

> *Though the work of the eldership is in itself very honorable and very interesting, yet it will be dull, formal, and worthless unless there is a real and growing love to Jesus in our hearts. That is the only oil that will make the lamp burn and keep it burning.*[11]

It is not an accident that most of Paul's list falls into this category. For this reason, those who desire to be in ministry should labor diligently to grow in these qualities, knowing it is the grace of God and the transforming power of the gospel that empowers the growth.

---

10 Haykin, Duke, and Fuller, Soldiers of Christ, p. 174.

11 David Dickson, The Elder and His Work, ed. George Kennedy McFarland and Phillip Graham Ryken (Phillipsburg, NJ: P & R Publishing, 2004), pp. 30–31.

**Spiritual maturity**

Once again, this category of spiritual maturity could be used broadly to include most of the list in 1 Timothy 3, but we will focus on two qualities that specifically evidence it. First, a pastor must be "not a lover of money" (1 Tim. 3:3). Because his primary responsibilities are to preach and teach the word of God and to care for the people sacrificially, idolizing money would be a contradiction. Assessing a man's fitness here is not connected to his income or investment statement. Instead, it stems from his heart posture toward money. An inordinate desire for more, a lack of contentment, and an obsession with hoarding indicate a disqualifying love of money. A proper desire for the work of pastoral ministry will always work against a desire for personal, material gain.

Second, as the spiritual leader and doctrinal gatekeeper of the church, a pastor "must not be a recent convert" (1 Tim. 3:6), which implies a spiritually immature man should not enter this work. This requirement seems obvious for several reasons, but Paul gives a specific one in this text—lest "he may become puffed up with conceit and fall into the condemnation of the devil" (1 Tim. 3:6). The gravity of this calling precludes immature believers from entering into it as they could become enamored by the power of the position instead of seeing it as a sacrifice and service to God and his people. Pursuing this office also places a man on the front line of spiritual attack from the enemy, which is much more difficult for new believers to endure. Given the protection maturity brings, the New Testament calls for a local church to appoint and then follow a number of godly pastors/elders in a local church for accountability, fellowship, and accumulated wisdom (Tit. 1:5; Acts 20:28; 1 Pet. 5:1).

## COMMITMENT TO THE LOCAL CHURCH

No one wants a physician who finished medical school but lacks the knowledge and wisdom that comes from hands-on experience in practicing medicine to treat sick people. Likewise, no one wants a pastor with seminary training but without knowledge and wisdom gleaned from ministering to others within the context of the local church. Nor should a local church affirm a man for this calling who has not demonstrated the required desire and character through his involvement in that church. In other words, in order for a local church to give an external call, a man must demonstrate his internal calling within that church.

It is a disheartening and all too common occurrence for young men to spend years training in seminary while cut off from meaningful membership and participation in a local church. Despite what many seem to expect, the diploma and salary from his first pastorate will not magically yield love for the local church. Instead, affection for God's people and love for the local church grows from a commitment to her and a firm grasp that she is the primary means through which God is building his kingdom and accomplishing his purposes in the world.

Further, the members of a local congregation must observe an internal calling as a man exercises his gifts, and the context for this ministry is the ordinary activity of that body. As the church family examines a man in light of the scriptural qualifications, they watch closely for him to display preaching and teaching gifts publicly and privately, a genuine care for widows and orphans, hospitality, and a desire to share the gospel with unbelievers. While it's possible for a man to exhibit these traits sporadically, the ongoing life of the church will expose his true heart over time.

As a man uses his spiritual gifts in the local church, the Spirit will apply them to impact and produce fruit in the lives of the people in his church. God will use a man's teaching to sow fruitful seeds of the word into people's hearts; will use his kindness and gentleness to the elderly, the hurting, and the sick to encourage the fainthearted; will use his generosity to help a family in need; and will use his hospitality to minister to a lonely person. As the man impacts others in the local church through deliberate and intimate involvement, God will equip that local church to affirm his internal calling through an external call. This reciprocity of ministry is the natural means for building the church and for using the local church to invest in God's larger kingdom.

Scripture and church history sufficiently articulate the way a man identifies an internal calling from God to pursue the noble work of gospel ministry. In addition, these sources provide measures for the local church to evaluate men in their service and fruitfulness among them. A believing man—who zealously desires this work, is apt to teach, faithfully leads his family, exudes a godly, blameless, and spiritually mature character, and is observed by others as he serves in the local church—qualifies for this work and should receive an external call.[12]

## PERSONAL REFLECTION

***Brian:*** I was one of those not properly tested and trained by the pastors or the local churches to which I served in my early years of ministry. This led to confusion in my calling, painful mistakes made, and a misunderstanding of the meaning of the local church. Because of this, there were times my ability to persevere was questioned.

12 These four areas were originally published and are explored in greater detail in Prepare Them to Shepherd, written by Brian Croft (Zondervan, 2014).

However, God brought perseverance in my ministry through two means. First, I had an unquenchable desire for the work of the ministry that only comes from God. My strong internal call was not easily swayed. Second, in the absence of a local church testing and training me, I found some older pastors outside my church context who taught me, mentored me, and helped shape what would later become a greater understanding and conviction of the internal and external call. In God's kind providence, it was the absence of an external call in my life that eventually stirred in me such a deep desire, as a local church lead pastor, to provide this for others.

I believe this led to our local church of less than 100 members testing, training, affirming, and sending out thirty-two families into pastoral ministry or the mission field in the seventeen years I served there. God created a sending culture out of a conviction to raise men and women up for ministry. I profoundly believe it is when an internal call is nurtured by an external call that a man is best prepared to know himself, his gifts, and his weakness, and thus will be more equipped to persevere when difficulty comes in his ministry.

***James:*** Over the years, I've seen God use both aspects of pastoral calling to strengthen and solidify men in the ministry, including, and especially, me. While training for pastoral ministry in seminary, I was eager to abandon secular vocation and pursue full-time church ministry. Those years of waiting served to deepen my sense of longing for the work, the memory of which still encourages me more than two decades later. Alongside this growing desire, God has been gracious to affirm my gifts for the work through his church in formal and informal ways that stabilize my heart amid the trials and challenges of pastoral ministry.

Like Brian, I've also observed the healthy and unhealthy side of this dynamic in young men who aspire to pastoral ministry. Some pursue formal training and then a vocational position without a meaningful connection to a local church in the process. Even worse, some fail to develop a relationship with an older pastor who can mentor them through the process. The result is generally technically trained but ill-equipped men, who have theological knowledge but are devoid of the social awareness and practical wisdom required to shepherd well. This approach sidesteps the God-ordained method for identifying, affirming, and training men for pastoral ministry to the detriment of the men and the churches they will serve.

## CONCLUSION

The office of pastor is a high and noble calling, bringing unique joy and satisfaction to those who serve as under-shepherds for the Chief Shepherd. But not everyone should aspire to this work because it is reserved for those who qualify for it. This "need to qualify" requires that we look beyond our subjective, personal desires to the objective, observable criteria given to the local church. Those who know the man well, have invested in him, and have tested and trained him must have a strong voice in affirming his fitness for pastoral ministry. This dual calling—internal and external—provides a stable foundation for a man to enter, stay, endure, and thrive in ministry, as he can be confident he is living obediently under God's assignment.

2

# A CALL TO TAKE HEED

*Pay careful attention to yourselves and to all the flock, in which the Holy Spirit has made you overseers, to care for the church of God, which he obtained with his own blood.*
(Acts 20:28)

Pastors generally fail to persevere in ministry for two main reasons. First, the work brings a distinctive weariness because it is uniquely challenging. Second, pastors often maintain an unsustainable schedule over the long term. The pastor runs like crazy from sunrise to sunset, with little or no margin for the unexpected and with virtually no consideration for the toll this pace exacts from him physically, emotionally, mentally, and spiritually. In an incredible irony, most pastors pour themselves out for the care of others without regard for the need to care for themselves. God has woven the principle of reaping and sowing into the created order, and these situations display it. A pastor's life will yield consequences—at times disastrous ones—when he exhausts the boundaries of human weakness without proper attention to the need for rest and renewal.

We have watched marriages implode, men break down mentally and succumb to deep depression, stress induce strokes and heart attacks, and even men end earthly life by suicide. A common thread connects every one of these tragedies—a neglect of personal soul care. While many humans experience stress, pastors experience a particular brand due to the spiritual nature of their calling. This common denominator of soul neglect is pervasive among pastors despite the sobering warning that extends from the Israelites' example: "let anyone who thinks that he stands take heed lest he fall" (1 Cor. 10:12).

Caught up in the overwhelming and unending pressures of this task of caring for others, formerly humble men surrender to the temptation to live as if they have a supernatural reservoir of strength. While we have resurrection power through the indwelling Spirit, God will not remove weakness and frailty associated with our humanity until final resurrection on the last day. Faithful pastors possess a zeal and deep conviction to shepherd God's flock as under-shepherds until Christ returns (1 Pet. 5:2–4), and thus they fulfill this calling sacrificially and diligently. The obedient pursuit of fidelity to this calling, however, often creates unscriptural inattention to his own soul to the detriment of his health, his family's health, and his church's health.

Paul, however, guides the Ephesian elders in the opposite direction when he gathers and exhorts them in Miletus with powerful words, before sailing for Jerusalem with an eye to Rome. Luke records his counsel in Acts 20:25–32:

> *And now, behold, I know that none of you among whom I have gone about proclaiming the kingdom will see my face again. Therefore I testify to you this day that I am innocent of the blood of all, for I did not shrink from declaring to you the whole counsel of God. Pay careful attention to yourselves and to all the flock, in which the Holy Spirit has made you overseers, to care for the church of God, which he obtained with his own blood. I know that after my departure fierce wolves will come in among you, not sparing the flock; and from among your own selves will arise men speaking twisted things, to draw away the disciples after them. Therefore be alert, remembering that for*

> *three years I did not cease night or day to admonish every one with tears. And now I commend you to God and to the word of his grace, which is able to build you up and to give you the inheritance among all those who are sanctified.*

The moving scene culminates with them escorting him to the boat and bidding him a tearful goodbye following his stirring words. These Holy-Spirit-inspired marching orders establish one of the clearest models for pastoral ministry in all of Scripture. Verse 28 defines the pattern most succinctly: "Pay careful attention to yourselves and to all the flock." This single imperative—pay careful attention—comprises the undeniable core of this work. According to theologian Joseph Thayer, the basic sense is "to set a course and keep to it."[1] Translations vary slightly as they try to capture the thrust of this command with phrases like "Keep watch" or "Be on guard," but perhaps the best at conveying the sentiment is the old King James Version's, "Take heed." While the cultural context for modern-day ministry is far removed from first-century Asia Minor, our central task remains the same.

## PAUL'S PASTORAL PARADIGM

Once again, Paul's charge to this group creates a pastoral ministry model built around two commands:

1. Take heed to yourself
2. Take heed to all the flock

Few, if any pastors, would dispute that the second admonition to "take heed . . . to all the flock" (KJV) sits at the center of our

1 Joseph Thayer, Thayer's Greek–English Lexicon of the New Testament (Peabody, MA: Hendrickson, 2002), p. 546.

task as shepherds. Many pastors, however, are surprised to learn that the command to "take heed . . . unto yourselves" (KJV) is set equal to or higher than it. Grammatically, Paul places the call to keep watch over ourselves in the place of priority, making it a foundation for the second and more widely recognized command. Building from our grasp of these two commands, we established the foundational identity of our organization Practical Shepherding around three core areas that we call "The Pastoral Trilogy":

1. *The pastor's soul:* This emphasis examines and expands upon the command to "take heed . . . unto yourselves" by defining its essence and tracing its branches into myriad layers of spiritual, mental, emotional, and physical care. Obedience to this call is necessary for a pastor to thrive and persevere amid the unique challenges of the ministry.

2. *The pastor's ministry:* Taking up the more common command of Acts 20:28 to "take heed . . . to all the flock," this aspect speaks to the fullness of a pastor's ministry to lead, feed, protect, and care for the individual souls of God's flock entrusted to him.

3. *The pastor's family:* While not expressly mentioned in Acts 20, this facet of life and ministry is vital for either encouraging a pastor or producing catastrophic, disqualifying failure. The blessing of a wife and children comes with the responsibility to prioritize caring for and shepherding them. For the man who desires to qualify for the office of pastor, embrace God's call to care for his sheep, and thrive in this work, faithful care of his family is essential.

These three areas capture the essence of the admonition for pastors to "take heed . . . unto yourselves, and to all the flock." Even more, they cast a healthy vision not only for simple perseverance but for thriving in ministry. Consider the potential ramifications for a pastor, his family, and his church if he neglects one or more of these critical areas.

Imagine the pastor who thrives in personal soul care and in ministry to the flock while his marriage is in shambles. The façade of this circumstance will eventually collapse. Similarly, a pastor thriving in his ministry and his family life at the expense of personal soul care will be crushed under the weight of the pressures of ministry. The dark clouds of depression may overwhelm him to the point that he struggles even to get out of bed. This scenario makes it impossible for a pastor to last long in pastoral ministry. Regardless of a pastor's gifts and abilities, neglecting the pursuit of health in all three of these core areas will have a detrimental effect on the man and the ministry.

The aim of this chapter is to present these three core areas of a pastor's life and ministry, explain how they flow from Paul's command to take heed, and demonstrate what it looks like practically for a pastor to live them out.

## THE PASTOR'S SOUL

The command to "pay careful attention to yourselves" (ESV) becomes a warning for all pastors about the dangers of neglecting our spiritual health. Most directly, this verse warns about the hazards presented, among the elders, by false professors who teach false doctrine. Paul warns, "And from among your own selves will arise men speaking twisted things to draw away the disciples after them" (v. 30). Lest any are lured into believing this is a hypothetical scenario, we could recount numerous tragic stories from personal experience. Even more, church history is replete with examples that illustrate the dire need for a pastor to watch out for himself.

What, then, does it mean for a pastor to take heed to himself? Looking elsewhere in the New Testament, we find Paul similarly exhorting Timothy to "Watch your life and doctrine closely" (1 Tim. 4:16, NIV). The latter part of this succinct counsel addresses the necessity of giving careful attention to what he believes because this will inevitably steer what he preaches and teaches. But he speaks first to the character of the man and the manner of his life, as we considered in the previous chapter. Without exception, a pastor's ministry will be marked by how well his life matches the gospel he proclaims.

Our experience, however, is that there are additional layers related to this imperative that are vital for helping a pastor thrive in his ministry. Under the umbrella of this command, consider the spiritual, emotional, mental, and physical aspects of care that affect a man's ability to persist in this labor. We will summarize our approach to acknowledging and addressing these layers in three headings: a personal walk with Jesus, an embracing of personal weakness, and a commitment to self-care.[2]

### A personal walk with Jesus

Certain foundational elements must define and describe the spiritual awakening of every pastor because their absence so often predetermines his demise. As we noted in the previous chapter, a man devoting himself to the task of shepherding—preaching, counseling, visiting, and leading—in the church must first be transformed by the power of the gospel. We would add to this basic requirement that he must also continue walking in fellowship with Jesus every day. In the realization of his constant

---

2 This section is further expanded in *The Pastor's Soul* written by Brian Croft and Jim Savastio (Evangelical Press, 2018).

need for Jesus, he should be turning to him in faith daily through spiritual disciplines, especially prayer and Bible study. Through this Spirit-empowered pursuit of Jesus, the man knows and is known by him. In addition, he grows steadily in love for Jesus as he longs to experience intimacy with him. Confident that he is forgiven by Jesus, he cries out to him in moments of weakness and desperation, believing he is always heard. The bedrock relationship for any pastor is the one he has and cultivates with his Savior and Lord.

Growing out of and supplying fuel for his relationship with God, the pastor must also love God's word. God's word forms the foundation for all of life because only through it can we accurately know him and know how we are to live in his world. Thus, it is central to every aspect of our lives, from the spiritual to the physical. Long before a man would ever presume to preach to God's people, he must devote himself to study the Scripture so that he may know God and what he has revealed to us. Knowledge, however, is not nearly enough. He must grow to love it by learning to feed on it, allowing it to nourish his soul.

Finally and correspondingly, the man who walks with Jesus and loves God's word must grow to love God's people. This characteristic is both an outflow of the previous work and a fruit of the Spirit. This genuine affection for God's people stimulates a commitment to sacrificially serve them, even at great cost, so that they come to know, love, and follow Jesus themselves. Love for God's people cannot be ascertained by osmosis through formal affirmations like ordination, magically conferred along with a Master of Divinity degree, or even deposited along with a paycheck from a church. Instead, this love sprouts in the man who clings to Jesus as Savior and humbly submits to the transforming work of the Spirit by the word of God.

**An embracing of personal weakness**

Strength in weakness is one the classic paradoxes of the Christian life. Worldly wisdom dismisses the idea that a person is strongest when he is weakest. God delights, as we know, in upending the wisdom of the world with his true wisdom. This concept is captured clearly in 2 Corinthians where Paul refers to his request for God to remove a thorn in his flesh:

> *But he said to me, "My grace is sufficient for you, for my power is made perfect in weakness." Therefore I will boast all the more gladly of my weaknesses, so that the power of Christ may rest upon me. For the sake of Christ, then, I am content with weaknesses, insults, hardships, persecutions, and calamities. For when I am weak, then I am strong (2 Cor. 12:9–10).*

We (Brian and James) have a confession to make. While always affirming Paul's teaching here as true, we have spent most of our lives pretending as if strength and weakness do not and cannot co-exist. By God's grace, however, we are continuing to learn that this combination is a key for living courageously and in the freedom of the gospel. True strength comes from Jesus living in us, which relies on our acknowledgment and embrace of weakness, humanity, ongoing fight against sin, and total dependence on him. Coming to grips with inability takes courage, but it is the only path to finding the divine strength necessary for faithful, pastoral ministry.

Convinced of this necessity, you may ask, "How do I own my weakness and gain this gospel-empowering strength?" Consider these three realities.

First, pastors must acknowledge that we are sinners. While sin has been defeated and our bondage to it broken by the sacrificial death of Jesus, we will not fully realize this freedom until we are raised from the dead. Therefore, it is essential that we accept the weakness of our humanity in this ongoing battle against sin. While frustrating, the truth that we are not God is a precious, freeing truth to our souls that eliminates the self-imposed and false expectation of perfection. We are human, still wrestling with temptation, and often succumbing to it. This is by no means a call to embrace sin, but to live in the reality of our need for Jesus' forgiveness. A denial of this weakness leads to failure, not to spiritual strength.

Second, pastors must own that we are not perfect. Pastors love to declare the unique sinlessness of Jesus, yet many of these same pastors are crippled by a fear of failure. Devastated because they do not measure up to expectations set by themselves or by others, they respond with overwork or laziness. Some toil endlessly to live up to an unbiblical standard while others slothfully despair until they give up. We have great news: not one pastor is perfect. God never expects that we will do everything right. He knows we will fail, and he has already accepted us. We are clothed in Christ's righteousness, so we must recalibrate our expectations based on the reality of our situation. God requires faithfulness of his servants, not perfection.

Third, pastors must accept that we are physically frail. Pride at work in the pastor's heart can drive him to want to appear superhuman and unaffected by the realities of the Fall on our bodies. We can keep pressing on physically until we hit the wall. Part of embracing our weakness is the acceptance of our physical limitations. God has woven a rhythm of work and rest into creation, and pastors are not above it. We must learn to recognize when to work as well as when to stop and rest. This embrace of personal weakness leads naturally to the next area that helps us apply Paul's command.

### A commitment to self-care

Within the rigors of hectic ministry life, pastors commonly neglect the tangible and most basic means of caring for themselves. Based on our experience over the years, we recommend six areas of physical care that act as a gauge to when a pastor's soul is struggling.

1. *Eat:* We often rightly ask, "What do we eat?" or even, "How much do we eat?" But we would argue an equally important questions is, "Why do we eat?" Allowing stress to drive us to eat or to avoid eating is evidence that a pastor is not living under the pressures, demands, and stresses of his life and ministry in a healthy manner.

2. *Sleep:* Most men have a problem with stating the amount of sleep they need because they wrongly understand the need for sleep as a sign of weakness. To avoid the appearance of weakness, then, many shade the truth. Thinking biblically, however, we know that sleep is a necessary part of living as humans in God's world. This gift of rest reminds us that we are not God and refreshes our bodies to allow them to function properly. Getting the proper amount of sleep is therefore essential to thriving as a human being, and certainly applies to pastors.

3. *Exercise:* The benefits of physical activity are varied and well-documented. Of all these gains, pastors should appreciate that exercise presents one of the healthiest ways of dealing with stress, as well as one of the best strategies for avoiding unhealthy responses to stress such as overeating and overworking.

4. *Friendship:* We are both convinced that friendships between pastors is a lost piece of the puzzle to having a persevering ministry.[3] A pastor desperately needs friends, as does his wife. The unique calling of a pastor demands that we invest in relationships with other pastors because these relationships carry a sense of common understanding about our task. Such Spirit-empowered friendships not only encourage and enable pastors but also enable those under their care to flourish. Therefore, these relationships are not simply rooted in enjoyment and companionship, but rather are grounded in the necessity to care well for one's soul and survive long-term in ministry.

5. *Rest:* Because ministry never ends, pastors must find time to rest, refresh, and spend time away from the burden of their work. While connected to the daily need for sleep, this call to rest expands to urge pastors to take a day off each week and regular vacation time. Even more, resting requires more than time away from the church building and the cell phone. Pastors often fail to rest even in these moments because they refuse to lay aside the mental and spiritual burdens of ministry. True rest requires entrusting people and their situations to God and allowing the heart and mind a respite from the weight of leading, feeding, protecting, and caring for the people.

6. *Silence:* Perhaps the most common method of avoiding personal soul care is filling our lives with noise, busyness, and distractions. Pastors must find regular time for stillness, prayer, and quiet reflection. The spiritual

3 See *Pastoral Friendship: The Forgotten Piece of a Persevering Ministry* by Michael A.G. Haykin, Brian Croft and James Carroll (Christian Focus, 2022).

discipline of silence and solitude is an instrument God uses to speak through his word, provide awareness of our pain and struggles, minister his grace, and give spiritual help in our time of need.

If these six practical steps are followed, they will help a pastor thrive and persevere in the place of ministry God has called him.

## THE PASTOR'S MINISTRY

In Acts 20:29, Paul provides the reason for the command that pastors must pay careful attention to the people under their care: "I know that after my departure fierce wolves will come in among you, not sparing the flock." We can safely draw the weighty implication that this danger is always present. It is not a question of "if" but "when" the fierce wolves or enemies of God will come seeking the demise of God's people. With a prophetic voice and strong imagery, Paul declares with certainty that they "will come" to devour God's flock. Thus, he places under-shepherds among the flock to pay careful attention to them.

Peter's similar admonition for elders to "shepherd the flock of God that is among you" (1 Pet. 5:2) demonstrates a key aspect of this pastoral work. Much of the lack of perseverance among pastors because of burn-out and discouragement stems from a misunderstanding, misapplication, or complete disregard for this basic call of a pastor to shepherd the people in his local church. Instead of shepherding, pastors can act like business CEOs, organizational managers and administrators, conference speakers, facilitators, or constituency pleasers. Their day-to-day work may bear little resemblance to a first-century shepherd.

It is quite stunning how confused many pastors are about the role they are to play as the pastor of a local church, despite the clarity of the New Testament on the matter. This disconnect comes from the immense pressure felt from our culture to produce something quick and measurable and from a distinct lack of conviction regarding the Bible's clear instruction about ministry.

Allow us to join countless others in church history in setting the record straight. This exhortation for the Ephesian pastors to "Take heed . . . to all the flock" can be more fully understood through two other biblical passages that address this topic:

> *So I exhort the elders among you, as a fellow elder and a witness of the sufferings of Christ, as well as a partaker in the glory that is going to be revealed: shepherd the flock of God that is among you, exercising oversight, not under compulsion, but willingly, as God would have you; not for shameful gain, but eagerly; not domineering over those in your charge, but being examples to the flock. And when the chief Shepherd appears, you will receive the unfading crown of glory (1 Pet. 5:1–4).*

> *Obey your leaders and submit to them, for they are keeping watch over your souls, as those who will have to give an account. Let them do this with joy and not with groaning, for that would be of no advantage to you (Heb. 13:17).*

While we will dig more deeply into what it means to "shepherd the flock that is among you" in the next chapter, we will outline here the broader pattern of the pastor's work. In pulling these two profound passages together, we can summarize God's design for this noble task in this way:

> The call of a pastor is to shepherd the souls of God's flock among them (1 Pet. 5:2) in the awareness that he will give an account to the Chief Shepherd (1 Pet. 5:4) for every individual soul under his charge (Heb. 13:17).

Pause to let that sink in. Pastors, we are not called to be CEOs, managers, motivational speakers, or facilitators. We are divinely appointed by the Chief Shepherd as under-shepherds, caring for the souls that were purchased by Jesus Christ as he laid down his life for them. Having bought them by his blood, Jesus now calls some from among the sheep to take the responsibility of caring for the other precious souls until he returns to gather all of them to himself. This is the pastor's ministry.[4]

To fulfill the ministry faithfully, pastors must be generalists. The average pastor serving fewer than one hundred people will play the role of "jack of all trades" over the course of their ministry by helping to meet spiritual and practical needs as they arise. All aspects of the pastor's ministry, however, fall under the umbrella of the shepherding of souls. Based on the numerous passages throughout the Bible that define and describe this task, we have developed ten priorities for pastoral ministry that we will treat fully in the next chapter. For now, that list is:

1. Guard the truth
2. Preach the word
3. Pray for the flock
4. Set an example
5. Visit the sick
6. Comfort the grieving
7. Care for widows
8. Confront sin
9. Encourage the weaker sheep
10. Identify and train leaders

---

4 This section is further expanded in *The Pastor's Ministry* written by Brian Croft (Zondervan, 2015).

These ten actions fit undeniably under the umbrella of the one central task—shepherding souls. We call them priorities because pastors will feel the pressure and often face the necessity of doing a wide variety of tasks beyond this list, but they should focus here whenever possible. We are convinced that a major contributor to the lack of pastoral perseverance stems from pastors spending most of their time doing everything but what they are commanded by God to do.

Therefore, a viable solution to empower pastors to persevere in their place of ministry is to help them return to the fundamental work of their calling. From Paul's admonition in Miletus to Peter's exhortation to his fellow elders and to the writer of Hebrews and his closing words about this work, the shepherding of souls is this central work.

## THE PASTOR'S FAMILY

The pastor's twin tasks of giving careful attention to his own soul and to the shepherding of God's people naturally flow out of Paul's imperatives in Acts 20:28. This final aspect of the pastor's life that completes our trilogy brings both imperatives together to concentrate on the pastor's family. In one sense, this call is part of the first two, but we have found it important to separate it out for emphasis and clarity. The pastor's wife and children are members of the flock under his care so they are already souls for which he will give an account to Jesus. Thus, caring for them falls under the command to take heed of his flock. Because of their vital, intimate connection to the pastor, caring for them also is an extension of caring for himself. Thus, taking heed to himself will naturally include shepherding those in his home.

There are unique dynamics at play within the pastor's family that demand a level of self-awareness, self-reflection, and attentiveness to make them a priority in a pastor's life. The unfortunate reality is that many pastors neglect their families for the sake of their ministry and, in incredible irony, have no idea they are neglecting the most fundamental place for that ministry. Even pastors who declare their commitment to prioritize their wife and children will sometimes fail to back that declaration up with actions that demonstrate it. For a pastor to thrive and persevere in his place of ministry he must "take heed" to himself and the flock in such a way that directly impacts his family.[5] Three scriptural principles shape our perception of a pastor's responsibility to his family.

First, caring well for his family is a prerequisite for qualifying as a pastor. Paul asserts this when describing a qualifying man as one who is faithful to his one wife (1 Tim. 3:2) and who manages his household well (1 Tim. 3:4). Correspondingly, he gives a principle that highlights the necessity of this requirement: "If someone does not know how to manage his own household, how will he care for God's church?" (1 Tim. 3:5). Before a man can be considered as a pastor, he must demonstrate care for his family in faithfulness to his wife and leadership of his children.

Second, a pastor is called to model to the church he serves faithful obedience to God. Peter exhorts pastors to be "examples to the flock" they are called to shepherd (1 Pet. 5:3). While broad in its application, this must necessarily include a pastor's life and leadership in the home. Therefore, the commands from Ephesians 5 regarding a man's love for his wife and from Ephesians 6 regarding his training and correction of his children become opportunities to live in an exemplary way before his church. These standards for Christ-likeness in marriage and family life should be observable in the pastor. While not a perfect

5 This section is further expanded in *The Pastor's Family* written by Brian and Cara Croft (Zondervan, 2013).

model, a pastor is called to set an example of God-honoring love and care for his wife and children.

Finally, every pastor will first give an account to Jesus for the souls of his wife and children. This principle comes to light when we consider the way Hebrews 13:17 aligns with the qualifications of 1 Timothy 3. If the call of a pastor is to give an account for every soul under his care and a qualification for a pastor is to care first for his family, then the combination of these two texts presents a plain and powerful truth—pastors will first answer to Jesus for their family.

Hopefully, the explanation and application of these biblical texts convinces you, but we will close this section with an appeal to your gut instinct. Dearest brothers, you know the unique challenges that await your family in this ministry. Ministry is hard for you and is particularly grueling for them. As an act of love for them, be sure to care for them well. Regardless of your gifts for and commitment to this ministry, their perseverance is necessary for yours. If you examine closely the statistics on the mass exodus of pastors from ministry today, you find quite often that family matters are at the forefront. For a pastor to thrive and persevere in his place of ministry, he must prioritize the care of his family. Practically speaking, several steps can be taken to this end.

To begin with, pastors must avoid using ministry demands and pressures as excuses for the neglect of their families. Pastors neglect their families for the same reason any man neglects his family—sin in the heart. Refuse to spiritualize your disobedience and own your sin. Confess and repent to them and to God when you fail to properly prioritize your family. Ask God to apply the transforming power of the gospel to help you pivot away from a sinful tendency in this regard. While they will be called on to sacrifice with you for the sake of service to God and his church, avoid placing them behind unnecessarily busy ministry life.

Next, care for your wife. Listen to her when she shares her concerns with you as she is the barometer of your marriage and family.[6] Receive her concerns with humility and grace, empathizing with her when she struggles with life as a pastor's wife. Watch and study her to know how to serve, encourage, disciple, and pray for her. God will use a supportive, discerning, and unimpressed wife to help bring balance and wisdom to a pastor's life and ministry—if only he will have eyes to see and a heart to appreciate it.

Lastly, shepherd your children. Family worship is a wonderful practice and discipline in every family's life, and especially in that of a pastor. In addition, we advocate making it a weekly habit to invest individual time with each child in your home. This time alone will allow you to see a glimpse into each child's heart that is more difficult when the whole family is present. In the same way we give time and energy to the individual soul care of each church member, we must invest in shepherding the little ones in our own home for as long as the Lord places them there.

## PERSONAL REFLECTION

***Brian:*** Paul's final words to the Ephesian pastors are clear. That is why I feel deeply about the need for this holistic approach to help pastors thrive and persevere in their place of ministry. But I also feel deeply about these areas because in my twenty-five years as a pastor, I learned many painful lessons in all three categories—a pastor's soul, ministry, and family. As my ministry was flourishing, my family imploded.

6 A barometer measures pressure. This metaphor highlights the unique role a wife plays in a pastor's home. That is, a wife possesses a Spirit-filled ability to discern the effects of ministry in the home often in ways the pastor cannot see as clearly.

But by God's grace and with some professional help, my marriage and family were put back together. My soul has had seasons of suffering horribly, which eventually led to a mental, emotional, and physical breakdown that required many years of counseling and medical care. And I spent several early years of ministry working an unhealthy, demanding schedule with tasks largely not involved in shepherding the souls of the flock.

I personally experienced the need for all three of these areas to be addressed and remain healthy in order for myself to persevere as a pastor. There is no way I would have been able to continue in my ministry without the grace of God intervening and addressing each area in my greatest times of need. I could not have continued in my ministry without beloved friends saying hard things that God used to get my attention. But these struggles do not have to have the last word. An eventual thriving in all three of these areas led to the opportunity to finish my local church ministry after twenty-five years and transition to leading Practical Shepherding, which I am hopeful will become the next twenty-five years of my ministry.

***James:*** The verb in Acts 20:28 that forms the basis for this chapter appears in the present tense in the original language. Greek students will know this conveys the sense of ongoing or continuous action. While I may have needed language study to tell me that a couple of decades ago, personal experience has served to confirm and solidify it. Giving careful, proper attention to my soul, my ministry, and my family requires concerted energy and constant dependence on the Spirit. Because of my weakness and frailty, relying on yesterday's work or coasting on yesterday's fuel are recipes for disaster.

The road of church history is littered with the record of men who started well, ran for a while, and then drifted or crashed along the way. Perseverance in this calling requires Spirit-empowered and persistent attention to the three aspects of life we have outlined. Like any tripod, they yield stability and strength when held together. But when any one of the three fails, the whole is doomed to fall with it.

## CONCLUSION

Parting words can be so powerful. With much that could be said but fleeting opportunity, often the most meaningful messages are delivered in these tender moments. Paul's final words to the Ephesian elders he knew and loved so well certainly fit this description. His summary of their pastoral responsibility in these two commands—to take heed to yourselves and to all the flock—creates a pattern for all who follow in their steps. As the modern pastor seeks to receive and apply these words, we hope he will consider his own soul, his own family, and his God-assigned task as an under-shepherd.

3

# A CONVICTION TO SHEPHERD

*So I exhort the elders among you, as a fellow elder and a witness of the sufferings of Christ, as well as a partaker in the glory that is going to be revealed: shepherd the flock of God that is among you. . . . And when the chief Shepherd appears, you will receive the unfading crown of glory.*
(1 Pet. 5:1–4)

Busyness marks life in our present culture. Some wear it like a badge of honor while others try to avoid it like the plague, but no one escapes it. The work to be done, people to contact, possessions to maintain, activities to schedule and attend, friendships to cultivate, guests to host, and appointments to keep are endless. Regardless of age and interests, most people have more to do than can reasonably be done. When Christians add meaningful participation—including regular worship attendance, volunteer service, and special events—to the list of normal busyness, their calendars fill to the point of bursting. Life in twenty-first century Western culture feels like an unending rat race that only slows down when crisis or sickness force it to a screeching halt.

Pastors not only observe the pressures, demands, and responsibilities that push and pull on church members, but experience them firsthand. Because the pastor's call to shepherd God's people requires involvement in their lives, he must juggle his own schedule with the added pressure of working around the hectic schedules of God's flock. The convergence of all this busyness creates expectations that bring tremendous tension for those in pastoral ministry, which sets them up for failure from the start.

This pressure yields two traps that sabotage perseverance. In some cases, a pastor quickly realizes that he cannot provide adequate care for his congregation, so he fails to attempt it. Even with a smaller congregation, it's impossible to attend *every* surgery, ball game, funeral, doctor's visit, home invitation, ministry activity, church workday, and counseling request. Discouraged, they stop trying altogether. While some languish in laziness, most redirect their attention to focus more broadly on administrating large activities, managing busy programs, and overseeing the practical functioning of the local church, leaving the work of "relational ministry" to others—or neglecting it altogether.

On the other hand, some determined pastors recognize that they can't do it all, but they commit to pushing through the pain to do as much as is humanly possible. They set an ambitious hand to the plow, hoping that with enough effort they can please at least *some* people. This approach is fraught with dangers, too. Now enslaved to the demands and needs of his church, the pastor allows the congregation to dominate his life. Whether directly or indirectly, other people's desires largely determine the investment of his time and energy. The measure of his ministry faithfulness and fruitfulness becomes intertwined with the congregation's expectations and his ability to meet them. While some are pleased some of the time, none are ever fully satisfied, and most find a reason to criticize him regardless. Pursuing human approval will inevitably lead to exhaustion and emptiness.

## A CONVICTIONAL CALLING

While called to fulfill a robust ministry, the pastor is tasked by God neither to run programs for the masses nor to satisfy every expectation. God, who alone can set men aside for this ministry, has the authority to establish the terms and responsibilities of their calling. Thankfully, he outlines the pastor's marching orders in his word. The pastor's path to steadfast faithfulness, which avoids the pitfalls of distraction and misdirection, is to know and do *what* God has truly called him to do. Peter exhorts elders/pastors[1] to shepherd—care for—God's people when he writes:

> *So I exhort the elders among you, as a fellow elder and a witness of the sufferings of Christ, as well as a partaker in the glory that is going to be revealed: shepherd the flock of God that is among you, exercising oversight, not under compulsion, but willingly, as God would have you; not for shameful gain, but eagerly; not domineering over those in your charge, but being examples to the flock. And when the chief Shepherd appears, you will receive the unfading crown of glory (1 Pet. 5:1–4).*

To summarize the pastor's calling in a single sentence, "Shepherd the souls of God's people under your care until the Chief Shepherd appears." Note the who, what, when, and how of this important work.

> *What:* Shepherd the flock of God.
>
> *Who:* The flock of God that is among you.
>
> *How:* Not because you must, but because you are willing, as God would have you; not pursuing dishonest gain, but

1 The New Testament uses the terms pastor, elder, bishop, and overseer interchangeably to refer to this one office of the pastor/shepherd.

> eager to serve; not domineering over those entrusted to you, but being examples to the flock.
>
> *When:* Until the Chief Shepherd, Jesus Christ, returns for his flock placed in your care.

A pastor's true calling, then, is to shepherd the souls of God's people humbly, willingly, and eagerly, and on behalf of the Chief Shepherd, Jesus Christ. Despite sweeping cultural changes that make life today quite different than in the first century, this task has not changed since the time Peter wrote these words. The basic responsibilities of pastoral ministry remain.

God's word is sufficient to equip a man for every good work (2 Tim. 3:17), including the work of pastoral ministry. The Scripture outlines the responsibilities of this divine calling and instructions for the man's daily priorities. Drawing on shepherd imagery, the Bible consistently highlights the central concerns for faithful pastors as leading, feeding, protecting, and caring for the souls of God's people entrusted to your care. In the face of the unbiblical demands, pressures, and expectations foisted upon a pastor that often crush his spirit, we hope studying and meditating on the biblical directives will solidify a conviction concerning the what, the who, the how, and the when of pastoral ministry.

The aim of this chapter is to highlight those scriptural priorities God sets for men who shepherd the souls of his people. He established them in the life of Israel, rooted them in his full redemptive plan, and confirmed them in the instructions given through Jesus and his Apostles. We have distilled the pastor's assignment into ten key biblical priorities, together with practical suggestions for engaging in each of these areas faithfully and fruitfully.

### Guard the truth

A pastor must be committed to Scripture by holding fast to it as the inerrant, infallible, sufficient, and living word of the living God. He must use it to preach, teach, lead, and protect God's people from the winds of confusion and temptation that swirl from godless cultural influences. As the Apostle Paul exhorted Timothy, pastors guard the deposit of sound gospel words that have been entrusted to us (2 Tim. 1:14), and then entrust them to other faithful men to do likewise as the truth carries on through successive generations. Pastors, then, are the doctrinal gatekeepers of the church, as they have been throughout church history. Paul captured this idea in his instructions to Titus pertaining to elder qualifications when he wrote that a man must be "able to give instruction in sound doctrine and also to rebuke those who contradict it" (Tit. 1:9).

Practically speaking, pastors guard the truth in the daily grind of ministry by first declaring the gospel regularly in the life of their church. We ought to clearly articulate the good news of God's plan and work to save through Jesus Christ in our sermons, songs, and prayers, both in public and in private. Second, pastors must demonstrate an unwavering commitment to truthfulness and usefulness in all of Scripture. To this end, preaching through entire books of the Bible will prevent shying away from difficult passages and demonstrate confidence in passages that draw hostility and rejection from contemporary culture. Finally, pastors guard the truth by employing God's word as the blueprint for leadership meetings, the basis for ministry philosophies and methodologies, and the foundation for church policies and procedures. When the truth undergirds and permeates the whole of church life, it creates a word-centered culture that breathes spiritual life into the church.

A pastor can fill his day with a variety of good labors, but they must be grounded in and driven by a conviction to steward God's truth by proclaiming the gospel of Jesus and teaching the whole counsel of God. Pastors and church leaders who fail to fulfill their calling this way, will build their ministries with "wood, hay, straw" that will be 'burned up" on the last day (1 Cor. 3:12–15). If we forfeit the truth, we will fail in our work. However, if we guard the truth, making it the lifeblood of our ministry, the Spirit will empower the work and use it to enliven the souls of God's people.

**Preach the word**

Growing out of our commitment to guard the truth, faithful pastors preach the whole counsel of God's word. They carefully explain the meaning of the text and make appropriate application to the members of their congregation. Perhaps the clearest of all pastoral imperatives from the Apostle Paul is recorded in 2 Timothy 4:2: "Preach the word." This ministerial priority was modeled by the Apostles in the early church. As the church's practical needs grew and problems arose related to the proper care for widows, they refused to relegate preaching to others. Instead, they identified and appointed other faithful men for these other tasks, so they could remain devoted "to prayer and to the ministry of the word" (Acts 6:4).

The urgency to preach as a key to pastoral perseverance provides the basis for our next chapter, but here we focus on the necessity of preaching to fulfill our task of caring for souls over the course of a long ministry. To this end, consider two specific applications. First, preach expository sermons as your church's regular, steady diet. Topical sermons have a place in pastoral ministry, but biblical exposition is the best way to teach the Bible and to teach people to read the Bible. Even more, systematic exposition through a single book of the Bible adds another layer of depth for instructing believers in the lifelong pursuit of knowing God through his word. Second, preach the word faithfully with longevity as your goal. Many young pastors succumb to the pressure of delivering a home-run sermon every week. They become enamored with trying to match the richness and impact of their favorite conference message in every sermon. However, the goal of pastoral ministry is steady saturation of the word over quick scriptural downpours. Borrowing from the baseball metaphor, God will use a persevering, faithful ministry of singles and doubles over decades to strengthen and stabilize his people.

God continues expanding his kingdom through the faithful proclamation of his word by his appointed messengers. Preaching was the central instrument God used to give birth to the church, to increase her throughout Jerusalem, Judea, and Samaria, and to establish her beyond the Roman empire. Likewise, God continues to build the modern-day church, to display his glory, on the faithful exposition and application of his word. As Jesus promised, God will build his church as his Spirit breathes life into his people by his lifegiving word, "and the gates of hell shall not prevail against it" (Matt. 16:18). A pastor, armed with this conviction, and moved by the Spirit in his mind, heart, and soul during his preparation, will preach the word with contextual awareness and deep passion. As he prepares with his unique church family on his mind, the Spirit will empower him to offer particular lifegiving instruction, exhortation, and admonition. And he will deliver the sermon as if life and death, heaven and hell, hang in the balance.

### Pray for the flock

Prayer is not an optional add-on to or a last resort for the pastor's ministry. The Bible is replete with direct commands to pray and more subtle implications of its necessary place in our lives. For example, we are called to be, "praying . . . for all the saints" (Eph. 6:18) and to "pray without ceasing" (1 Thes. 5:17). Rather than directly commanding his disciples to pray, Jesus assumes it by introducing his teaching with the phrase, "when you pray . . ." (Matt. 6:5–7; Luke 11:2). As in other ways, pastors set an example to the flock (1 Pet. 5:3) by modeling prayer, both publicly and privately.

With a conviction to pray firmly established, the pastor fulfills the role of intercessor by bringing before God the needs of the flock entrusted to him. To ensure he prays regularly for every soul under his care, it is wise to create a systematic way of praying for every member in the church on a regular basis. One time-tested strategy divides the membership roll into twenty-eight groups and assigns a group to each day of the month. Along with praying for each member family, the pastor can call, email, or text at least some of those families to encourage them by sharing that you prayed for them. Additionally, this prayer calendar can serve as a shepherding checklist, allowing you to care for the sheep and prevent any from wandering away.

We cannot overstate the privilege pastors have to intercede for the needs of God's flock through Jesus' mediating work. Their reconciliation has been fully and completely accomplished through the life, death, and resurrection of Jesus, who now sits at the Father's right hand making intercession for all who have been transformed by the gospel by faith in him. Because we are beneficiaries of this redeeming work ourselves and called as his under-shepherds, we are honored to follow him by interceding for everyone in our church. In addition, we follow the ministry of the Spirit by interceding for believers according to the Father's will. While we cannot know all that God is purposing for them, we can pray for their sanctification and perseverance.

As stewards of this flock, without the ability to meet their needs, we bring them to the Chief Shepherd. Involving others, especially fellow elders, in this work allows us to rejoice together in our full access to God through the perfect mediating work of our Redeemer and in his answers to these prayers.

**Set an example**

Pastors live with the awareness that their congregations are directed to consider them as models (Heb. 13:7). Even more, the Apostle Peter exhorts pastors to be "examples to the flock" (1 Pet. 5:3) and Paul reminds younger pastors they too are not exempt from this responsibility (1 Tim. 4:12). While modeling righteous behavior, a pastor must also display a pattern of confession and repentance that acknowledges his remaining struggle with sin and demonstrates how to apply the gospel in daily life.

This priority of setting an example presents an interesting paradox for pastors. On the one hand, they are called to live as models of faithfulness and godliness. On the other hand, they are sinners who struggle with sin, fail to walk perfectly by faith, and make unwise decisions. Thus, they need Jesus' help through the ministry of the Spirit the same as anyone. While some pastors will sin to the point of disqualification, even the faithful will stumble at points along the way. Because the calling is not to perfection, pastors can be an example of humility and sanctification by confessing sin, repenting, apologizing to others, asking for forgiveness, admitting wrong, and pursuing reconciliation. A pastor who models this kind of transparency for their flock will have an even more fruitful ministry among them.

Being up-front is an extraordinary honor for pastors. Not only are we beneficiaries of the example of others—those who faithfully led us, spoke God's word to us, and powerfully lived that word in front of and with us—but we now can do the same for those under our care. May the weight of this encourage you to lay hold of God's power in the gospel rather than crush you under unbiblical expectations. By God's sustaining grace, pastors can persevere in steadfastness and faithfulness, running a race for all to imitate.

**Visit the sick**

While our ministry extends to every member of the church, we bear distinct responsibility to care for the hurting and afflicted among us. To this end, pastors should visit those who are sick and in need of special care and encouragement, and they must train others in the congregation to help in this work. Jesus taught that this responsibility falls to all who follow him when he said, "I was sick and you visited me" (Matt. 26:36). Even more, the expectation that pastors will lead the way is seen in James' instruction that a church should call the elders to come and pray for the sick (Jam. 5:14). Additionally, times of crisis and struggle in a hospital room provide pastors with key shepherding moments by ministering comfort through tenderness, Scripture, and prayer.

Pastors commonly avoid making these visits because they are fearful or uncomfortable about what to do or say. We will offer a few practical tips from our experience to help. First, take your Bible and read Scripture to them, allowing the word of God to fill the silence. Second, pray with them, specifically pointing to the hope we have in the gospel. Third, engage the person in conversation by looking them in the eye and smiling as appropriate for the circumstance. Fourth, plan to stay only briefly—no longer than five to ten minutes—so your visit is not a burden. Fifth, greet family members present in the room and ask how you can serve them. Sixth, remind the person and the family that they are loved by the church. Finally, if the person is unavailable or resting when you arrive, leave a note behind with scriptural encouragement.

The disciples' basic command to love others as ourselves extends especially to those bound with us in our local church. As we enjoy fellowship with those present from week to week, it can be easy to lose sight of and even forget those unable to attend for a long period. The temptation is to allow encouraging them to slip soundlessly through our schedules. In the face of this, pastors must take the initiative to know the struggles of their people and to meet them in their affliction. Through this divine task, souls are nurtured toward eternity on behalf of the Chief Shepherd. As the gospel is proclaimed, the church is edified, and God is glorified.

**Comfort the grieving**

In the face of death, a pastor must grieve with those who grieve and remind them of the hope and encouragement of the gospel, with sensitivity and grace. The primary instrument of comfort at our disposal is a gospel-drenched sermon delivered in funeral and graveside services. While the Bible contains many passages that are perfectly suited for these situations, perhaps the best is John 11, the record of Jesus' ministry following the death of Lazarus. This narrative provides a pattern for preaching funeral sermons because it raises the three main points that comfort grieving people with the hope of Christ.

First, Jesus weeps at the tomb of Lazarus. This detail reminds the hearer of their need to stop, embrace their sorrow, and grieve. It also highlights Jesus' compassion for hurting people, and it powerfully demonstrates his humanity as he is moved to tears despite his knowledge of the imminent miracle of resurrection. Second, Jesus uses this tragic circumstance to declare his identity. He announces in his conversation with Martha, "I am the resurrection and the life. Whoever believes in me, though he die, yet shall he live" (John 11:25). Knowing that he would defeat death, he explains that his resurrection is the path to victory over death for all who are united to him. Finally, Jesus asks Martha a rhetorical question, "Do you believe this?" (John 11:26), which allows a pastor to invite all who are mourning to lay hold of Christ by faith, not merely for comfort in grief but for forgiveness of sin and salvation.

Pastoral tenderness and biblical teaching are critical but wearing the cap of an administrator and facilitator is necessary throughout the process. These skills help us maneuver the details and demands that accompany funerals with deftness and sensitivity. We must prepare and conduct funerals in the knowledge that these grieving families are hurting and longing for tender care. Therefore, shepherd them by reminding them both to grieve as well as to turn to Jesus in faith as he is their only hope.

**Care for widows**

Caring for the widows of the church is a much-neglected biblical teaching for pastors in our present moment. The Bible consistently highlights God's heart for the widow, and the New Testament gives guidance on how pastors can lead the church to carry out this vital ministry. Remember that this issue caused the Apostles to lead the believers in Jerusalem to identify and appoint seven godly men to serve the widows in need (Acts 6:1–7). In addition, Paul equips Timothy for leading the church in this ministry by instructing him on who the widows are, how to identify them, and how to specifically care for them (1 Tim. 5). Therefore, pastors are both accountable for overseeing the widows' care (according to 1 Tim. 5), and must follow the example of Acts 6 to lead the church in taking on this responsibility. To this end, the congregation should ask non-pastors to direct this ministry and find creative ways—often involving families and multi-generational groups—to care for such widows. Even though the task does not fall solely to the pastor, he must play an important role in this ministry.

Unfortunately, widows are not typically vocal in fighting for their pastor's time. Thus, pastors must take the initiative to prioritize participating in the care of these precious members of the flock. The care of widows is often not difficult, but it requires an investment of time and intentionality. First, visit them in their home. This step helps to address one of their greatest snares: loneliness. Second, whenever possible, include widows in your family celebrations—birthdays, Thanksgiving, and Christmas. Many widows have few living family members of their own, and others who have living children are often separated from them by distance. Finally, honor the memory of their deceased spouse by remembering anniversaries, both of their wedding and the spouse's death. Never forget that modeling this type of ministry can equip and encourage others to care for widows in the same ways.

If pastors want their ministry to mirror the heart of God and the ministry of the early church, then caring for widows is essential. Understanding the commands and personal obedience are a great place to start, but proper, effective care for widows requires thoughtful evaluation of the unique needs of each widow and congregational commitment to meet them. In obedience to the Great Shepherd, prioritize this important work for the sake of the sheep and for the joy of this rewarding ministry.

## Confront sin

Pastors must confront sin and lead the church to exercise discipline in the hope of repentance and restoration. This work is difficult and often painful, but it is the undeniable command for the New Testament church. Jesus describes the steps for confronting a brother who has sinned against you in the hope of reconciliation (Matt. 18:15–20). Likewise, Paul instructs the Corinthian church in responding to someone engaged in unrepentant, public, scandalous sin (1 Cor. 5:1–5); he counsels Titus on dealing with divisive people (Tit. 3); and he teaches the Thessalonians regarding believers who take advantage of others (2 Thes. 3). These instructions require a firm hand but must be carried out with love and patience to pursue the blessings and benefits of restoration.

Faithfulness in this painful task is, first, obedience to Scripture, which is always a blessing for God's people. By leading in discipline, the pastor serves the church well. Second, confronting an unrepentant sinner who professes to follow Christ defends the name of Jesus. The church must protect his name by exposing any attachment of sin. Third, exercising church discipline protects the church from the ongoing effects of this outward display of disobedience. Finally, this work contributes to the fulfillment of the pastor's purpose, namely the care of souls. Faithful pastors must pursue straying sheep who are in danger of falling away.

Pastors are called to shepherd the souls of God's people, and there may be no more essential aspect of that calling than confronting them in habitual, unrepentant sin. If done according to the prescriptions of Scripture, the result is often the joy of seeing a wandering saint return home again. Sometimes, we see no immediate, visible fruit, and tragically, some who go astray will never return. In those times when temptations to discouragement come, cling to the Bible's promise that God is pleased by under-shepherds who lead their churches to pursue wayward sheep, in obedience to his word and for the sake of his great name.

**Encourage the weaker sheep**

Moses' ministry of leadership in the wilderness unmistakably demonstrates that shepherding God's people is a challenging charge because of human weakness, both in them and in us. Though it is tempting to dismiss difficult people, God calls pastors to model patience and persevering hope by working with those who struggle to make spiritual progress. Because weakness is common to all people, we must be careful not to form negative opinions about or label people who are despairing in their circumstances or presenting challenges for the church. Paul identifies some believers as "the weaker brethren" in a couple of New Testament passages (Rom. 14 and 1 Cor. 8–10) and instructs the church to minister tenderly to them. For example, he directs the Thessalonians to "encourage the fainthearted, help the weak, be patient with them all" (1 Thes. 5:14).

Because this pastoral priority is often hard, exhausting work, steadfastness in it requires the Spirit's enabling and sustaining power. For a pastor to continue in faithfulness, he must approach it patiently as weaker believers often make progress more slowly. In addition, he must fulfill this work with hope, trusting that the Holy Spirit is at work even when he can't see it. It is also vital that this work is not done alone. The trap of believing that the pastor is the only one who can help this group presents a real temptation. To combat it, commit to involve others and share the burden.

Pastors who give precedence to this difficult but important aspect of shepherding and fulfill it faithfully will not only see weaker brothers and sisters encouraged and built up, but the local church will be more equipped to honor Christ by obedience in all areas. Additionally, these congregations normally grow in compassion, empathy, and hope because of their experience in seeing God work among some of the most vulnerable sheep.

**Identify and train leaders**

The scope of a pastor's ministry ought to extend well beyond his present field and even his earthly life. By identifying, raising up, training, and affirming leaders in the local church, the seeds of his gospel labor will reap a harvest long after he is gone. Every pastor should have a plan for doing this in his local church and should be actively seeking the next generation of leaders. A biblical template for this training and sending ministry is seen in the Antioch church when it affirms and sends out Saul and Barnabas on their first missionary journey (Acts 13:1–3). Well before seminaries, Bible colleges, or mission organizations were established, the local church and her leaders carried out this vital task. After investing in their lives and ministries for years, the church identified them through prayer and sent them out. As the narrative in Acts recounts, this church continued to play an active part in their remaining missionary ministry.

Many local churches and pastors today shirk this responsibility, assuming others will do it, but it remains their task. This process of identifying and training up men for service in pastoral ministry follows four steps: Test, train, affirm, and send. In leading this charge, pastors test the desire and gifts of men who desire this ministry. Second, and part of this testing, they train them for the work of pastoral ministry by instructing, modeling, and releasing them to do the work under their supervision. Third, and after testing and training, the pastor must lead the congregation to evaluate the man so they can affirm his calling when appropriate. Finally, the church sends the man when they are confident in his pastoral or missionary calling.

We cannot emphasize this step too much nor commend it too highly. For the sake of the church of the future, carve out time for this vital aspect of ministry. Pastors play a unique role in recognizing another pastor. Look persistently and graciously, acknowledging the potential candidate's apparent maturity, and discern whether he exhibits a commitment to spiritual growth and the gifting to teach God's word and care for his people. Even without a formal process for identifying and training men, a pastor can invest in this individual. For example, he can join in visits to hospitals, nursing homes or those confined to their homes, and when ready, he can lead and teach in the church's normal ministries.

As the pastor engages in this work informally, he can begin teaching the congregation about the church's responsibility to identify and train candidates for gospel ministry and church leadership until a formal process is in place. If pastors do not accept this role and make this a priority, the church rarely will. Although this task is often ignored by busy pastors, they will answer for failures to train and equip the next generation of leaders as Scripture prescribes.

## A FINAL CAVEAT

At first glance, these ten priorities omit other important aspects of a pastor's ministry such as evangelism—as Paul exhorts Timothy to do in 2 Timothy 4:5—and caring for the poor—as he instructs the church in Galatia in Galatians 2:10. These other responsibilities are important and necessary for the health of any local church, and they are areas in which a pastor must lead, model, and encourage his church. However, we focused on the priorities of a *shepherd's* ministry or the aspects pertinent to his care for God's people in particular. Even though we have not directly addressed many important ministries, they are woven throughout the ten priorities. Evangelism is an aspect of preaching the word, guarding the truth, and comforting the grieving, and caring for the poor is an inevitable component of visiting the sick, caring for widows, and encouraging the weak.

## PERSONAL REFLECTION

***Brian:*** As I came to realize God was calling me to be a shepherd of souls, it produced two things. First, it increased my joy in the ministry work I was doing. God did not call me to run programs and events, but to care for people's souls. While the conviction to shepherd souls was already there, I was being asked to do other things. But my true desire when I accepted a call into pastoral ministry was to shepherd souls, and it brought a tremendous amount of joy in my life once I finally was able to engage in it. That has been an important asset as I sought to persevere in my ministry call.

Second, it was a very freeing experience to learn my task was to shepherd souls. The burden of organizing programs and events felt empty and hallow. The burdens that come from caring for others were of a different nature and one I gladly embraced. Although it is very difficult at times to care for hurting people, I find it a gift and privilege to be a part of people's lives in their key moments.

***James:*** Despite two decades of pastoral ministry, working with Brian to compile and explain this list is as convicting as it is encouraging. Of these ten priorities, some more naturally flow from my disposition and extend from my gifts, while others I find more challenging. As such, it can be tempting to give primary energy to some and neglect others, but none are optional, and all must be pursued with Spirit-empowered effort. In addition, myriad activities and events distract from these priorities and threaten our concentration on them. Knowing these aspects of our calling is vital, but it's only the beginning. I pray God will strengthen men to comprehend and commit to these critical labors.

## CONCLUSION

Pastors feel the burdens and pressures of ministry and deal with impossible expectations. Ultimately, we want to free them from the bondage of trying to meet every need and do too much, losing valuable time on less important work and maintaining countless unappreciated, head-spinning tasks. Rather than succumbing to these unbiblical demands, our hope is that God will enlighten pastors by the power of his word to know God's design for life and ministry, embed in them a conviction to shepherd souls, and give discernment for fulfilling this ministry. Pastors who persevere understand their task to shepherd souls, embrace it as their true calling, and live with awareness of their accountability to the Chief Shepherd. Only in surrendering to God's design and plan for ministry are they able to press on, endure whatever comes, and thrive where God has placed them.

# 4

# AN URGENCY TO PREACH

*I charge you in the presence of God and of Christ Jesus, who is to judge the living and the dead, and by his appearing and his kingdom: preach the word; be ready in season and out of season; reprove, rebuke, and exhort, with complete patience and teaching.*

(2 Tim. 4:1–2)

Many readers have likely heard the story of my (Brian) seventeen-year pastorate. The first five years were brutal. When I arrived, this Southern Baptist Church consisted of thirty elderly people on the southside of Louisville, Kentucky. The virtually non-existent ministry was matched only by the church's finances. Although I did not know it when I was hired, they could only afford to pay my salary for about six months, and even without the commitment to my compensation, they were headed toward closure in two to three years. The situation actually deteriorated after my arrival. I faced three different efforts from within to fire me in those first five years.

The first of these attempts happened only three months into my ministry, and it was initiated by a staff member I had inherited. He boasted of getting my predecessor fired, and he tried to do the same with me. The second firing attempt came at the two-and-a-half-year mark when I led them to find the 580 people on the membership roll who had not been to church in over ten years. I will never forget receiving the phone call warning me about these maneuvers while I was on a family vacation. The third—and thankfully final—firing attempt arose at the five-year mark and ultimately led to an exodus of twenty-five percent of the congregation. Some of the folks who left had come under my ministry during the previous five years and had become dear friends. When the smoke cleared, I was beat up, discouraged, and ready to leave.

As I look back, I persevered in that field for two reasons. First, I sensed God, in faithfulness to his church, would not abandon us after bringing us so far. We could identify evidence of his grace and work, even in the midst of the hostility. Second, I was haunted by the words of Hebrews 13:17 and the realization that I will give an account for every soul under my care, even those who didn't like me very much. So, I stayed, along with some of the hostile members. In that sixth year God displayed his power and grace in turning the ship. This change of course led the church to flourish over the next decade.

The church grew numerically and, more importantly, spiritually. We adopted a church leadership structure that included the two biblical offices of pastors/elders and deacons, and we affirmed men to serve in these roles who grasped their scriptural responsibilities and excelled in them. We celebrated conversions among the people in our neighborhood. We experienced ethnic diversity that mirrored our community, having previously been a multi-generational but all-white congregation. This diversity even included refugees. The change was not only inwardly focused but outwardly as we raised up pastors and missionaries and sent them out. Most significantly, the spiritual temperature of our gatherings shifted as the angry, scowling faces I had grown accustomed to seeing as I preached now softened. People who had been hostile to me began to trust me, and even grew to love me. They accepted my preaching in ways they had previously resisted and developed love for biblical exposition. I'm so thankful I stayed, and even more, I'm grateful for the previously hostile members who stayed with me. Our perseverance together laid the groundwork for God's sovereign, stunning work of redemption in the lives of a young, broken pastor and a discouraged, hurting people.

## PREACHING WITH A PATIENT URGENCY

Pastors encounter an apparent contradiction as they preach and minister in hostile environments. We believe the word of God is powerful enough to build a church and breathe life into cold hearts and dying churches. Because of this conviction, we approach sermon preparation and delivery with commitment and seriousness. Facing hostility at the outset often serves to reinforce our urgency, causing many men to pour themselves into ministering God's word with fervor.

Despite the power and sufficiency of God's word to create life by reviving the dead, he rarely hurries to complete his work, based on our measure of time. He always acts, but rarely as quickly as we would want. In fact, according to Jesus' parables in the gospel accounts, God's design for building his kingdom is intentionally slow, subtle, often hidden, and generally unimpressive. Herein lies the profound paradox related to God building his kingdom through the preaching of his word: While pastors should sense an urgency for his work, God contentedly plays the long game. Understanding this idea helps the pastor balance his urgency to preach with the necessary patience to wait for God to work on his timescale. Jesus captures this concept so well in the parable of the sower:

> *Again he began to teach beside the sea. And a very large crowd gathered about him, so that he got into a boat and sat in it on*

*the sea, and the whole crowd was beside the sea on the land. And he was teaching them many things in parables, and in his teaching he said to them: "Listen! Behold, a sower went out to sow. And as he sowed, some seed fell along the path, and the birds came and devoured it. Other seed fell on rocky ground, where it did not have much soil, and immediately it sprang up, since it had no depth of soil. And when the sun rose, it was scorched, and since it had no root, it withered away. Other seed fell among thorns, and the thorns grew up and choked it, and it yielded no grain. And other seeds fell into good soil and produced grain, growing up and increasing and yielding thirtyfold and sixtyfold and a hundredfold." And he said, "He who has ears to hear, let him hear."*

*And when he was alone, those around him with the twelve asked him about the parables. And he said to them, "To you has been given the secret of the kingdom of God, but for those outside everything is in parables, so that*

*they may indeed see but not perceive,*
*and may indeed hear but not understand,*
*lest they should turn and be forgiven.*

*And he said to them, "Do you not understand this parable? How then will you understand all the parables? The sower sows the word. And these are the ones along the path, where the word is sown: when they hear, Satan immediately comes and takes away the word that is sown in them. And these are the ones sown on rocky ground: the ones who, when they hear the word, immediately receive it with joy. And they have no root in themselves, but endure for a while; then, when tribulation or persecution arises on account of the word, immediately they*

> *fall away. And others are the ones sown among thorns. They are those who hear the word, but the cares of the world and the deceitfulness of riches and the desires for other things enter in and choke the word, and it proves unfruitful. But those that were sown on the good soil are the ones who hear the word and accept it and bear fruit, thirtyfold and sixtyfold and a hundredfold" (Mark 4:1–20)*

Because Jesus interprets this parable, we have no doubt about its meaning and significance. The sower's seed is God's word (v. 14). Like natural seed, it falls on different kinds of soil that receive it with greater and lesser success. When it finds the good soil of a receptive heart (v. 20), it takes root, germinates, and grows, even yielding a massive harvest. God's word is powerful, and he uses the spreading of it to build his kingdom.

The metaphor unmistakably conveys deliberateness that can feel like downright slowness. Farming does not deliver a quick return. Everything about this example reinforces patience and dependence on God. After the seed is scattered, the sower is helpless in speeding up the rooting and growth process. He must wait to see if the seeds produce sprouts, let alone a fruitful harvest. The incredible sight of produce comes only after the long and grueling process of growth.

Jesus teaches a number of valuable lessons in this simple parable. It reinforces both that the word of God builds the kingdom of God and that we can trust that God's timing always perfectly accords with his purposes. Sowers of the word must be faithful to play their part, and then wait for God to do his work by his Spirit. Jesus exhorts pastors to patience.

This balance of urgency and patience is a difficult and critical aspect of persevering in a preaching ministry. While most pastors begin with a tremendously eager resolve, the most common reason they fail to persevere stems from a lack of patient endurance in the absence of visible results. In the parable of the sower, Jesus clarifies that urgency without patience is not his design, and often leads to discouragement and despair. The power of God's word does not guarantee it will act quickly. This period of waiting leads many pastors to frustration, questions of personal effectiveness, doubt in God, and a wavering commitment to his word. All this can culminate in the pursuit of another foundation for ministry or another field of ministry. In contrast, pastors who persevere in a hostile ministry post embrace both urgency and patience in their preaching.

## PREACHING WITH URGENCY THROUGH HOSTILITY

The animosity toward my (Brian) ministry during those five years was evident every week in angry, scowling faces in the congregation. The church's dismissive posture toward the pulpit was connected to a broader lack of confidence in the pastoral office resulting from a thirty-five-year pattern of two- or three-year pastorates. A more direct factor in their lack of appreciation for my preaching, however, stemmed from the fact that my sermons were so vastly different from what they had previously experienced. The seventy-five-year-old church never had a pastor with a commitment to preaching an expository sermon. Their steady diet of preaching for over half a century matched that of the typical Southern Baptist Church—evangelistic, topical preaching with a strong influence from the Billy Graham Crusades.

Upon arrival, I began preaching expository sermons through books of the Bible, and it was not received well. Critics pejoratively defined my sermons as more Bible Study than preaching. I remained convinced that this pattern of verse-by-verse exposition of his word best embraces God's design for breathing life into a church, and so I plodded along week after week. In those first five years, some members grew frustrated and trickled away because of their dissatisfaction. However, God honored the slow, steady preaching of his word to grow the church numerically and spiritually by winning some long-time members and drawing others from outside the church.

At the five-year mark of my pastorate, 85% of the pastoral committee who hired me had either died or left frustrated, particularly with my preaching. This exodus included, in year three, the key member of the committee who arranged my initial interview. She wrote me a letter explaining that my expository sermons provided the reason for her exit. Her letter became a needed catalyst for improving my sermon delivery, which suffered because of my failure to engage the congregation effectively while preaching from a manuscript—though I had done so because I wanted to carefully and accurately communicate the message. Those early years frustrated me and the congregation in part because, as a rookie preaching pastor, I was finding my voice as a weekly expositor. Despite a conviction that God's Spirit uses his word to build a healthy church, young, inexperienced preachers must work to hone their craft and develop their gifts. So while unflinching in my determination to preach urgently and through expository sermons, I renewed my commitment to grow as a preacher.

Persevering in this ministry was extremely difficult. However, in God's kind providence, he taught me the biblical formula for persisting, and even bearing fruit, while preaching in a hostile environment. Again, this answer flows from the paradox of preaching with urgency and patience. The formula is simple—preach and stay.

## PREACHING AND STAYING

The biblical formula for surviving and bearing fruit in pastoral ministry, especially in hostile situations, is to preach and stay. Before expounding upon this formula, it is important to dismiss two harmful preaching strategies that are popular today but damage both the pastor and the congregation.

First, some pastors will *preach and leave*. Many pastors go into a struggling church and labor week after week to preach thoroughly biblical and helpfully practical sermons with passion. However, incorrectly assuming that God's power in and through his word is the guarantee of rapid change, they quickly grow frustrated. Discouraged by their unmet (unbiblical) expectations, they leave for another church hoping it will be different.

Second, some pastors capitulate to the congregation's criticism and *don't preach, but stay*. Rather than committing to continue preaching patiently, they lose confidence in God's word. Borrowing from the empty well of pragmatism, they decide expository preaching will not bring life to the struggling church. The urgency to preach the word evaporates and these pastors either turn to topical, lighthearted sermons or abandon preaching altogether. Not wanting to offend and devoid of assurance in the role God's word plays in spiritual formation, they chase quick-fix strategies promised by gimmicks, entertainment, and even self-help philosophies. In the name of pleasing people for numeric increase, they fail to please the One who matters most.

Unfortunately, neither of these methods will bear fruit, and both will inevitably harm the flock. Therefore, the biblical formula for pulpit ministry in hostility is to preach and stay.

## Preach

Paul's well-known exhortation to Timothy provides one of the clearest commands for pastors found in the New Testament. In what is commonly believed to be his final letter, he wrote:

> *I charge you in the presence of God and of Christ Jesus, who is to judge the living and the dead, and by his appearing and his kingdom: preach the word; be ready in season and out of season; reprove, rebuke, and exhort, with complete patience and teaching. For the time is coming when people will not endure sound teaching, but having itching ears they will accumulate for themselves teachers to suit their own passions, and will turn away from listening to the truth and wander off into myths. As for you, always be sober-minded, endure suffering, do the work of an evangelist, fulfill your ministry (2 Tim. 4:1–5).*

The central imperative reveals the baseline strategy for building a local church—preach the word. In addition, the text helps the pastor know how to apply and execute this charge faithfully. Paul offers the:

- *What:* I charge you to preach the word (vv. 1–2)
- *When:* In season and out of season (v. 2)
- *How:* Reprove, rebuke, and exhort with great patience and instruction (v. 2)
- *Why:* A time will come where they won't want it (vv. 3–4)

These descriptions, especially the call to patience, contribute to our confidence that persevering in difficulty is central to the pastor's task. The four additional exhortations—"to be sober-minded, endure suffering, do the work of an evangelist, fulfill your ministry" (v.5)—that close the paragraph reinforce the priority of preaching and the likelihood of suffering. Every faithful pastor, whether in the first or the twenty-first century, must "preach the word" with a sober mind and the resolve to persist in suffering, which is an unavoidable result of hostility.

**Stay**

Thankfully, many pastors preach faithfully, and our experience confirms that most of these men do so boldly in hostile environments. However, too few of them endure through suffering and difficulty despite the biblical formula to preach *and stay*. Paul conveys this crucial piece at the end of his letter to the Corinthians:

> *I will visit you after passing through Macedonia, for I intend to pass through Macedonia, and perhaps I will stay with you or even spend the winter, so that you may help me on my journey, wherever I go. For I do not want to see you now just in passing. I hope to spend some time with you, if the Lord permits. But I will stay in Ephesus until Pentecost, for a wide door for effective work has opened to me, and there are many adversaries (1 Cor. 16:5–9).*

Even though Paul wants to visit Corinth again, he explains two important reasons for his staying in Ephesus.

For starters, his work among the Ephesians is not yet done. Paul altered his plans because he realized God had opened a wide door for effective ministry where he was. His commitment to submit to God's leading overrode his desire to see the Corinthians and continue his ministry to them. Though a missionary and frequent traveler, Paul understood the value of remaining in one place when the situation warranted it.

A second reason Paul gives for staying is the presence of many adversaries. This rationale seems backward in our day when pastors often conclude the presence of adversaries and hostility is evidence that God is leading them elsewhere. Paul functioned under a completely different paradigm. Because of his love for the flock and his desire to protect them, he understood opposition as an indicator that he should stay.

The biblical formula to survive and even thrive in a preaching ministry that faces hostility, then, is to preach the word and stay. Pastors persevere in faith, trusting that God will build the church on his word and staying long enough to give persistent, passionate preaching time to bear the spiritual fruit God has promised. In other words, they preach with urgency and patience. Keeping his hand to the plough, a pastor may have the privilege of rejoicing when snarlers and scowlers become attentive hearers and joyful recipients of the word.

## FIVE LESSONS FROM PREACHING WITH A PATIENT URGENCY

By God's grace, I (Brian) was patient, staying long enough to see this kind of spiritual fruit. Eventually, the weight of hostility turned to joy. Looking back, I can identify five key lessons about preaching with urgency and patience I learned along the way. Had I abandoned my post in impatience or compromised my commitment to preach expository sermons, I would have missed the joy of the harvest. I'm thankful to God for his strength enabling me to preach and stay. While forged in the furnace of my trails, these five principles can help a pastor in any situation to remain steadfast.

**Solidify your conviction that God's word builds the church**

It's easy for seminarians and young pastors to launch into ministry zealously declaring they believe the word of God builds the church, but they can lack commitment to it in practice when they begin pastoring a struggling local church. This dissonance is revealed when they focus too much on the various dysfunctional aspects of their church's ministry and lament her resistance to change. Emboldened by a sense of self-righteous arrogance in knowing what ought to be done but hamstrung by the congregation's tradition or distrust, their frustration boils over. Some proceed undeterred by the opposition, feeling justified because their aims match the biblical designs for a local church, but the results are often catastrophic. Most of these pastors are fired or leave under duress.

A pastor must resolve to address the most important need in the church and to wait to address the less critical problems. He has the biblical authority and mandate to exert his leadership immediately regarding what comes from the pulpit each Sunday. A pastor who believes the word builds the church over the long haul won't ignore the other areas for needed growth, but he will be content to concentrate on his preaching ministry and leave the rest for later. This prayerful dependence on God to work through his word to build the church creates a resolve to preach the word and love the people.

**Listen to and learn from the criticisms of those who don't like your preaching**

In the early years, it's easy for pastors to think they are being patient. While enduring criticisms, judgments, and even direct attacks on them and their ministries, they can become convinced they are taking the high road as the bigger, more faithful person. They toil in the study and thunder in the pulpit, pouring out their hearts, only to receive scowls from the crowd. As we (Brian and James) have matured, however, we have come to realize the congregation demonstrated incredible patience with us. Long-time, faithful saints, who had been wounded by a succession of previous pastors over decades, specifically exhibited great patience with us as we developed as preachers.

Betty, a long-time member and a widow in her eighties, routinely offered criticism of my (Brian) preaching in those early years. Of all the people who didn't like my preaching, she was the only one with the courage and grace to tell me so and why. Like most young pastors, I immediately dismissed her evaluation. But as I matured as a pastor and preacher, she grew wiser every year. About eight years into my ministry, I suddenly realized I had incorporated many of her suggestions. Not only does she enjoy hearing this testimony, she now loves to hear me preach. In my final years of serving as her pastor, she regularly greeted me with tears after the sermon because of the way the word ministered to her weary soul. She represents many others who patiently persevered in my preaching.

Unsolicited sermon criticism is challenging to receive for a variety of reasons. Often the source is hostile and the delivery, harsh. But pastors do well to listen to people who don't like their preaching. As they preach with great patience and instruction, they ought not to underestimate the patience the congregation is exhibiting toward them. Even more, they must tune their ears to receive sermon assessment with grace because God generally uses it to sharpen their preaching gifts.

### Remember God's word never returns void—even when received through scowls

Flashbacks from my (Brian) early years as a pastor remind me of the difficulties I faced in preaching. The struggle came from both sides. I lacked confidence in my preaching, and my congregation lacked interest in my preaching. Few people ever brought a Bible, and almost no one used it. Many sat with folded arms and angry faces. To prevent this hostility from taking a toll during the sermon, I printed and taped the following message on the top of the pulpit:

> *You don't preach for the praise of man, but to declare the truth of God's word. It is enough and a worthy, noble work to preach God's word even if it is not received by the hearers.*

If your joy in proclaiming God's word depends on the response from your hearers, you won't last long in a hostile, struggling church. We must trust that God works through his word in our preaching in numerous ways, even and especially when we can't see it. Results are not our responsibility. Rather, we are called to preach and endure, entrusting the results to God. We "preach the word" with "complete patience" and to "endure suffering" (2 Tim. 4:1–5). Hostility toward preaching cannot alter God's purpose or thwart his work.

**Foster supportive but unimpressed evaluation of your preaching**

Pastors, like nearly everyone, seek affirmation and encouragement by surrounding themselves with supportive people. Shaded by their love for us, often this group view us unhelpfully and naively as the greatest preacher, the most compassionate counselor, and the strongest leader. Attraction to this support leads many to avoid less flattering feedback and criticism. While hearing only negative reviews can be stilting and discouraging, effusive praise is equally dangerous. The solution is to develop a system for receiving supportive but unimpressed evaluations of your preaching. Most often, a faithful pastor's wife can play a key role here. We (Brian and James) are both blessed with wives who fit this description.

- *Supportive*: A pastor's wife ought to know him better than anyone. She will know his struggles, faults, inadequacies, and sins. Yet, she should possess an unshakable support, love, affirmation, and care for him. She lends her support in all circumstances, including his greatest successes, most painful conflicts, greatest betrayals, and worst sermons. All pastors need this kind of backing, especially in hostile ministry atmospheres.

- *Unimpressed:* The wife's unwavering support contributes by stabilizing and strengthening a pastor, but viewing her husband and his ministry with rose-colored glasses can be equally detrimental. Because of her access to his life, she observes the blind spots of his life, ministry, and preaching most clearly to see the reality of his need for Christ and the gospel. Rightly discerned, this perspective produces a supportive but unimpressed wife, who can help her husband identify areas of pride and self-deceit as they emerge in his heart. When applied to his preaching ministry, she can listen objectively to him and offer valuable input to help him grow as a preacher. If she's too easily impressed by his gifts for ministry or if she overlooks his weakness, her praise can tempt him to ignore reasonable criticisms from credible people that could prove helpful.

When preaching in a hostile environment, the pastor needs unwavering support to buoy his spirit to persevere but also constructive evaluation to help him discern which assessments to receive and which to discard. For a variety of reasons, not every pastor's wife will fulfill this role. This task is not biblically required so a pastor must avoid placing undue pressure on his wife. If she cannot help him in this area, his need for "supportive, but unimpressed" evaluation of his ministry remains. Especially when preaching through hostility, he must pray for and seek out others who will help him in this way.

### Cling to knowing that there's nothing like a congregation who grows hungry for the word

Paul's instructions for Timothy to "preach the word . . . in season and out of season . . . with complete patience and teaching" highlight his confidence that over time the word will transform the people. My (Brian) first five years were brutal. The fights, conflicts, scowls, folded arms in the pews, attacks in the community, and attempted firings in the early years made the church a much sweeter place in the end. The joy of seeing someone, who once sat and scowled, receive the word and respond with tears of hope is indescribable. When Betty's post-service greetings morphed from criticism to big hugs and encouraging words related to the sermon, the challenge of those early conversations faded behind the glory of God's grace to both of us.

Imagine the shift from a church with little to no appetite for the word, seen in virtually no commitment to bring a Bible, to a congregation so hungry to feed on the word that every Bible reference brings a chorus of page turning and a unified posture of reading along in their respective copies. The Lord's work to bring change in a hard, hostile place enhances the sweetness of preaching to these sheep. While inheriting a healthy and thriving congregation is a blessing, it can't compare to the joy of watching a congregation grow hungry for the word over time. Preaching the word faithfully and patiently to a struggling, hostile church is God's path of kind transformation. He will breathe life into that church through his word over the course of years.

## PERSONAL REFLECTION

***Brian:*** As this chapter reflects on some painful memories in my ministry, I am reminded of how crucial it is to feel both the urgency to preach and yet the need to embrace patience. Some of the pain in my story was manifested when I felt the urgency to preach but lacked patience. Zeal without wisdom is dangerous. Passion without patience leads to bad decisions. Many battles I unwisely chose in my ministry, and which led to painful consequences, were often the result of impatience.

Likewise, it was discouragement, even despair, that crept in my soul when I embraced patience but lacked a purposeful urgency to preach. In my lowest moments, as I faced the unrelenting hostility to my preaching, I questioned whether this was all worth it. Urgency to preach fosters a purposefulness to our ministries, especially when we face adversaries. A lack of urgency crushes our resolve to press on. I am convinced as ever that it is an urgency to preach soaked in patience that provides the divine template to face any ministry struggle with purpose and steadfastness.

***James:*** My story of perseverance differs from Brian's quite a bit. I have faced very little of the hostility he describes throughout the chapter. However, in the early years of my current pastorate, some in the congregation responded to my preaching with apathy. Accustomed to topical sermons driven by felt needs, they shrugged with indifference at consistent biblical exposition. While many in the church quickly grew to appreciate and then love expository sermons, a contingent of folks voiced their displeasure and many left the church. At numerous points along the way, I was tempted to succumb to discouragement and abandon this commitment or this post.

Devoid of the excitement of dramatic conflict and open outrage, I describe my trial as more like the nag of a dripping faucet than the surge of a rushing river. I faced no tsunami of opposition, but the smaller waves of criticism just never stop. No individual wave is enough to overwhelm, but they *just never stop*. The symptoms may have been different, but the disease and the treatment are the same. My perseverance in preaching required first an urgency to give them the word every week, with this commitment solidified and stabilized by the Spirit's application of word to me. The second necessity was a commitment to stay that was reinforced by God's kind providence in countless ways.

## CONCLUSION

Brothers, persevere in your preaching! Embrace the urgent call to proclaim the good news of Jesus and boldly preach God's word. God will build his church. Correspondingly, embrace the call to stay. Exercise patience and steadfastness long enough to see spiritual fruit manifest from your preaching. Commit to stay through the difficulty and watch for God to bring life back into his church. Pastoral perseverance in a preaching ministry comes not from learning to preach home-run sermons or from the adoration of the congregation, but from a Spirit-empowered resolve to stay the course. Preach with urgency knowing the necessity of this task, and cultivate patience trusting God to bring his harvest in his time.[1]

1 Some of the concepts and ideas in this chapter are further expanded in the book Facing Snarls and Scowls by Brian Croft and James Carroll (Christian Focus, 2019).

# 5

# A TENACITY TO SUFFER

*And we know that for those who love God all things work together for good, for those who are called according to his purpose.*
(Rom. 8:28)

If church historians made lists like sports journalists do, many would argue that when it comes to preaching—outside Christ and the Apostles, of course—Charles Haddon Spurgeon is the GOAT. (If you're unfamiliar, that's an acronym for Greatest Of All Time.) He began preaching as a teenager and was almost immediately recognized for his extraordinary gifts, delivering more than six hundred sermons before turning twenty. At the age of nineteen, he became the pastor of the largest Baptist church in London, the New Park Street Chapel. The church grew rapidly and was forced to rent venues to hold the growing crowds. Seven years into his ministry, the congregation settled into a new permanent location and became the Metropolitan Tabernacle, where he ministered for the next thirty-plus years.

The reach of Spurgeon's preaching extended well beyond the five thousand people who filled this megachurch building. They translated his sermons into twenty languages and sold approximately twenty thousand copies weekly. He became known as the "Prince of Preachers." His collected sermons have been called "the largest set of books by a single author in the history of Christianity."[1]

Don't be misled. While the statistics make his ministry look like a breeze, it was anything but. Even outwardly fruitful ministries are not immune from trials and suffering. In fact, often the notoriety brings additional challenges. Like Paul, Spurgeon could have written about affliction "at every turn—fighting without and fear within" (2 Cor. 7:5). He faced nearly every form of adversity imaginable in one way or another.

Despite his meteoric rise and widespread popularity, he was often the subject of public criticism and ridicule. An article in the *Essex Standard* surmised: "All the most solemn mysteries of our holy religion are by him rudely, roughly and impiously handled. Common sense is outraged, and decency disgusted. His rantings are interspersed with coarse anecdotes." The attacks were so prevalent that his wife was able to compile a scrapbook of them from the years 1855 and 1856.[2] Twenty years later he remarked, "Men cannot say anything worse of me than they have said. I have been belied from head to foot, and misrepresented to the last degree."[3]

The attacks ebbed and flowed over the years until they culminated in his withdrawal from the Baptist Union over the Downgrade Controversy in the late 1880s. He took a firm stand against associating with those who refused to maintain doctrinal fidelity. The world's most well-known preacher at the time can now be recognized as a prophet, but he could not convince his brethren. They continued down their path and even voted to

1 Eric Hayden, "Charles H. Spurgeon: Did you Know?" (Christianity Today); https://www.christianitytoday.com/history/issues/issue-29/charles-h-spurgeon-did-you-know.html (accessed 25 October, 2018).

2 John Piper, *A Camaraderie of Confidence* (Wheaton: Crossway, 2016), p. 46.

3 Piper, A Camaraderie of Confidence, p. 47.

censure him several months after he withdrew. Adding insult to injury, his brother seconded the Union's eventual motion to adopt a compromised doctrinal statement.

Despite the obvious difficulty in all these situations, the one event that seems to have caused him the most grief happened on October 19, 1856. As he stood to preach before more than ten thousand people in the Music Hall at Royal Surrey Gardens, someone in the crowd yelled, "Fire!" In the ensuing chaos, seven people were trampled to death and dozens more injured. Many blamed him. The burden so overwhelmed him that he did not preach for months and even considered quitting. Decades later, the haunting memory would return like post-traumatic stress along with feelings of responsibility and guilt.[4]

Adverse life circumstances at home created burdens for Spurgeon as well. His wife, Susannah, gave birth to their twin boys in 1856, but they were not able to have more. Her health declined significantly in her mid-thirties to the point that she was rarely able to hear him during the last twenty-five years of his ministry.

The fighting without was matched by physical suffering within, in the form of gout, rheumatism, and Bright's disease. The onset of gout came in his mid-thirties and grew worse over the years, causing him to vacate his pulpit for months at a time to recover. When he died at only fifty-seven, he was in France attempting to recuperate from the ongoing maladies in his diseased and failing body.[5] This man with a sharp mind and booming voice was no superman, and reminders of his frailty were constant throughout his ministry in London.

4 Zach Eswine, "Charles Spurgeon (1834–92): Faithful in Sorrow" in 12 Faithful Men, ed. Collin Hansen and Jeff Robinson (Grand Rapids: Baker, 2018), p. 131.

5 Piper, *A Camaraderie of Confidence*, p. 46.

His inward suffering was not isolated to physiological matters; Spurgeon also wrestled with "spiritual sorrows." As pastor of the same church for thirty-eight years, he knew well the minor disappointments of shepherding unfaithful members and leading a large congregation. His "mental miseries" were much worse, though. The dark clouds of depression covered him first at the ripe age of twenty-four when he described his spirit as "sunken so low that I could weep by the hour like a child, and yet I knew not what I wept for."[6] This battle raged throughout his life, making him feel at times that God had deserted him and at others that God was smiting him.[7]

Despite all this suffering, Spurgeon endured to the end as pastor of the Metropolitan Tabernacle. While a casual glance at his life might lead to the assumption that he sailed through it untouched by the ordinary trials of ministry, any such thoughts are sorely misguided. But despite the intensity and variety of suffering Spurgeon experienced all throughout his life, he persevered until the end. Charles Spurgeon is celebrated for many of his accomplishments, but one of his greatest qualities—his grit and tenacity to persevere through unrelenting suffering—is largely overlooked and underappreciated. Beginning with his example, this chapter addresses the inevitability of suffering for every pastor, the plan of God for every pastor in suffering, and the means of developing a tenacity to suffer that empowers a pastor to persevere until the end.

## THE FORMULA FOR TENACITY

Younger generations of pastors experience two common challenges to perseverance before they even begin. First, they

6 Piper, *A Camaraderie of Confidence*, p. 48.

7 Eswine, "Charles Spurgeon", p. 129.

approach pastoral ministry with unrealistic expectations that leave them frustrated and disappointed when churches are not lined up ready to hire them after their recent graduation from seminary. Second, many have matured into adulthood with an inability to suffer with tenacity. Let's face it, no one wants to suffer because suffering is, well, painful. But unfortunate and adverse circumstances are necessarily part of life. Even more, they are central to the life of a believer. Jesus' reference to his followers' cross-bearing (Matt. 10:38) points in this direction, and Paul's encouragement to Timothy removes any doubt: "Indeed, all who desire to live a godly life in Christ Jesus will be persecuted" (2 Tim. 3:12). Thus, pastors who enter the ministry with the unbiblical expectation of an easy life devoid of suffering are set up for disappointment and/or failure.

The proper expectation certainly readies a man for the struggle, but it will not produce the grit and tenacity he needs. Instead, something greater and more meaningful must undergird a pastor as he strives to persevere for decades. God provides sustaining grace through two promises that come to us through Paul's pen:

> *And we know that for those who love God all things work together for good, for those who are called according to his purpose (Rom. 8:28).*

> *Blessed be the God and Father of our Lord Jesus Christ, the Father of mercies and God of all comfort, who comforts us in all our affliction, so that we may be able to comfort those who are in any affliction, with the comfort with which we ourselves are comforted by God. For as we share abundantly in Christ's sufferings, so through Christ we share abundantly in comfort too. If we are afflicted, it is for your comfort and salvation; and*

> *if we are comforted, it is for your comfort, which you experience when you patiently endure the same sufferings that we suffer. Our hope for you is unshaken, for we know that as you share in our sufferings, you will also share in our comfort (2 Cor. 1:3–7).*

Because of God's kind providence, all Christians can have confidence that the suffering we endure is never in vain. God unconditionally promises that he will oversee and direct all things in this life to converge so that those who love him, those he has called according to his purpose, experience ultimate good. While the reference to "all things" should be read comprehensively, the immediate context of Romans 8 emphasizes suffering and trials. In addition, the Corinthian believers know God's comfort in suffering, "so that we may be able to comfort those who are in any affliction, with the comfort with which we ourselves are comforted by God (2 Cor. 1:4).

Pastors, who are quick to preach and apply these promises to others, must consider their relevance for themselves. Instead, many modern pastors are surprised when adversity comes. Some pastors crumble at the first hint of it while others conclude adversity and adversaries are signs from God that they are in the wrong place. Pastors are not exceptions to the rule that God intends for his people to suffer for our good and his glory.

This formula for pastoral perseverance begins by pastors embracing the reality of suffering as God's plan in their life and ministry. Mental and spiritual preparation begins long before becoming a pastor and lays the groundwork for the tenacity to suffer well. We must learn, mediate on, memorize, and cling to God's promises. Exposure to other pastors' ministries will also allow aspiring pastors to see the joys and struggles of pastoral ministry. This approach will help them develop a deep, abiding faith in God's plans and purposes, which will strengthen their resolve to endure suffering. Even more, this resilience rests on the perspective that trials are God's gift to sanctify us and more firmly establish his church.

## ADVERSARIES AND ADVERSITY

Some churches and pastors carry a disproportionately heavy burden. The crises and tragedies in some fields seem exorbitant. We look back over years of ministry in our respective places in full realization that the seasons of blessings and moments of joy far outweigh the times of adversity. We provide these anecdotes to give current examples of the timeless theological truths we're highlighting, but neither of us would contend that our suffering is exceptional or especially noteworthy. We are ordinary men, serving in ordinary fields, facing ordinary adversity. However, reflecting on the categories of crises Spurgeon faced, we can offer a few examples.

When it comes to public criticism and ridicule, relatively few men know what it's like to have disparaging newspaper articles written about them. Yet, most of us have caught the swirling wind of criticism aimed at us. I (Brian) know this firsthand. I mentioned earlier the mass exodus of the pastoral committee that hired me, in large part because of my preaching. One of those committee members left making a lot of noise. She not only hated my preaching, but she grew hostile toward me over a couple of decisions I made that she didn't like. This led her to slander me and go out of her way to seek out other pastors to tell them how much she despised me. She then rallied her friends and family to help. Some of the things she said were true—I had made certain decisions. I can live with those things.

The slander, the lies, and the blatant efforts to mar my reputation around the community with untrue stories were much more difficult to endure. I remember walking into a community coffee shop and people who had never met me knew of me because of this well-connected women's demolition efforts to take me down. Similar experiences happened at the grocery store, bank, and funeral homes. Her family knew a lot of people and wanted me to know it.

Fighting outside the church is tough, but when the adversity invades the home it often takes on a greater intensity. These struggles might seem insignificant to others, but we'd liken them to surgery. As the saying goes, "The only minor surgery is the one someone else is having." Here are a few examples of adversity in our homes.

**No place to live**

The fall of 2013 was a roller coaster for our family (James). I was returning from a meeting of pastors in Nashville on a Wednesday afternoon in August when I received a call from a mentor and friend. He wanted to talk because he had just finished eating lunch with the chairman of a pastoral search committee during which they invested a significant portion of the time watching one of my sermons. "I would love to give them your résumé," he said, "but I need you to consider it and determine if God is leading you in this direction." I made no commitment, except that I would speak to my wife about it when I arrived home. She was neither impressed nor excited. I thank the Lord for her in so many ways and, in this case, for her immediate clarity on the ridiculous nature of that notion. I only entertained this opportunity as an escape hatch and not because God was moving me toward it.

We put that "opportunity" to rest within forty-eight hours and returned to normal life, only to learn about a week later that we would indeed be moving in the next few months. We had been renting a house from a church member for three years and, due to circumstances beyond her control, she needed us to vacate it. We appreciated her grace, sensed her agony, and felt for her. She remained a dear friend and church member until her death. There was no ill will, but the situation created a crisis for us. We weren't leaving Bardstown, Kentucky, but we were moving. Complicating matters, however, was the fact that we still owned a home in Georgia. The housing market crash of 2009 eliminated the equity in our home, forcing us to hold onto it and rent it out when we came to Kentucky in 2010. The prospects of buying a second home were bleak, but we quickly learned that the rental market yielded few options that fit our price range and needs.

For about five weeks, we scoured the market for available places and grew more anxious by the moment. At some point along the way, we determined it would be cheaper each month to pay a mortgage than to pay rent and focused our energies in that direction. In late September, we put down an offer on a house and negotiated for a few days, haggling over a couple of thousand dollars. The seller left town for a long weekend on a scheduled trip and we expected to close the deal without any problems when he returned. Relieved, we spent the weekend mentally decorating the home and making plans. The call from our realtor on Monday morning rattled me more than I'd like to admit. After receiving zero offers in eleven months, the seller received an offer higher than ours over the weekend and had accepted it. He provided no opportunity for us to counter. The deal was done, the house was sold, and we were back to square one.

To increase the tension, I was scheduled to leave the country that Saturday for Haiti. We discussed the wisdom of my going given the uncertainty of our situation, but decided I should keep the commitment. I boarded a plane on the last Saturday in September knowing that we would move before the end of October, but uncertain as to where we would go. The stress of the situation was great, but it did not compare to the inner strife produced by that eight-week period. The possible opportunity to leave, the failed attempt to buy a home, and the inability to find a place to go combined to create a burden that brought me to the brink of despair.

It may not seem like much in one way, but the threat of homelessness exposed the dangerous mirage of self-sufficiency in my heart and mind. Because my instincts seemed wrong at every turn, I began to doubt myself and wonder about God's care and control. The Lord's kindness showed powerfully in the weeks that followed. Not only did he provide abundantly for our physical needs, he sanctified me in the process. He exposed the absurdity of my self-sufficiency and proved his steadfast loyalty. It didn't feel like it at the moment, but that adversity was a gift.

**Identity crisis**

I (Brian) hit a horrible wall about ten years into ministering at my church. It was in a season where my ministry in all areas was flourishing. But my soul was dying. My marriage was struggling. My wife was in a dark place. I had run our family into the ground and had done the same to myself. So much of my mental and emotional breakdown was rooted in ministry becoming my identity. And I was terrified to face it. It took me almost losing it all to get help. Even then, I did it begrudgingly. God used a very wise and skilled counselor and some close, patient pastoral friends to take me on a long-needed journey. It was a very painful journey that shook my identity to the core and that began with seeing the reality of my weakness and humanity.

At my lowest moments I struggled to get out of bed in the mornings. My joy was gone, and it was a challenge to even accomplish my daily responsibilities. It was a journey to understand and embrace my weakness, trusting Jesus would meet me there—and give me strength. He did. I am still on this journey, but my life is radically different. My soul is at peace in a way I never thought possible. I have experienced firsthand that, in Christ, there is indeed strength when we embrace our weakness (2 Cor. 12:9–10). My identity crisis and adversity had almost cost me my ministry and family, but it was also an incredible gift from God that reshaped and reset the trajectory of them both. In the midst of it all, God was still building his church among us. It didn't feel like it at the moment, but that adversity was a gift.

**Seizures and slander**

Everything seemed to be humming along smoothly for us (James) as we neared the end of school in 2015. I first noticed something strange was happening with my son as we tossed a baseball in the backyard. Every now and then, he'd lose focus. All of a sudden, he'd drift mentally and completely disengage with what was happening around him for ten to fifteen seconds. At first, we shrugged it off as child-like daydreaming. He's the type of kid who can shut out the world when he concentrates, so we thought he was just hyper-focusing at inopportune times.

The situation continued to intensify, however, and we grew convinced that he might be suffering from a medical illness. Our pediatrician and personal friend advised us to keep an eye on him to note exactly what was happening and to schedule an appointment in a week or so. That space of time was important for us to monitor him closely, but it was excruciating as we watched him suffer. After a brief medical exam, his doctor made an initial diagnosis that shocked and scared us. While he referred us for neurological testing to confirm it, his opinion was that our son had a form of epilepsy and that he was suffering from absence seizures. Within a week, further testing and consultation from the neurologist confirmed it and our son started taking medication. As others whose children have faced illness and disease will know, the ground beneath us was not stable. In the grand scheme of medical possibilities, this diagnosis could have been much worse, but the weight of that struggle was indescribable.

By God's providence, the day I took my son to his appointment with the pediatrician, I was called into another meeting. A member of our church had contacted the office to ask about a letter she received in the mail that day. The typed, anonymous letter was a slanderous attempt to discredit me personally and disparage my ministry. With an unknown number of letters circulating, a few of our leaders wanted me to know about it and to express their support. That week, which included a sleep-deprived EEG for my son, also included leadership meetings to discuss the veracity of the letter and the appropriate response. The ministry burden couldn't compare to my concern for my son, but it added to the size of the trial.

God's provision and care for us during that week was extraordinary. When we look back, we can see how he was planning for and orchestrating events to care for us more than two decades prior. The letter is a distant memory and my son, by God's grace, has not had another seizure since the Monday that followed that first appointment with the pediatrician. It didn't feel like it at the moment, but that adversity was a gift.

**Matters of the heart**

At the height of church conflict, while I (Brian) was trying to survive the third firing attempt in five years, I had a health scare. I started to have anxiety attacks as well as heart palpitations. When they got bad it was scary because they would take my breath away for a moment. They got bad enough that I eventually had to go to the doctor, who hooked me up to a heart monitor so they could observe what was happening.

As my doctor was seeking to find what was wrong, he casually asked, "So, how much stress are you under?" I was a bit taken back by his question, so I responded, "Well, about as much as everyone else who is pastoring a church and has a young family, I guess." I downplayed the hostile church environment I had lived in for the last half decade. Then he asked something that God used in a powerful way: "Did you know most research agrees you have one of the most stressful professions anyone can have?"

That was the first moment the dots began to connect. The stress from the last five years could be the cause of my heart issues. I was the classic example of the frog in boiling water and I had missed the connection. Not anymore. I began to care for myself in a different way. I started taking all my vacation time. I realized I had limitations and I needed to listen to them if I wanted to be able to minister well into the future. I started listening to my body to grow in awareness of the emotional and mental stress in my life. It didn't feel like it at the moment, but the adversity caused by the hostile church environment was a gift.

**Seasons of sorrow**

The final example of adversity for me (James) to share comes with no story. It is not an event. I would describe it as despondency. It seems to be much less than what is often called depression and yet more than simple discouragement. It's not an overwhelming sadness, but a recurring melancholy that erodes my joy. Certainly, circumstances play a role, but are not the overriding cause in all cases.

The struggle is not constant, but it is persistent enough. It comes like a fog to encompass my heart and mind, at times without warning. When a day or a moment seems bright and my heart is resting content in God, a hint of fear or dread will invade to capture my attention. Then the encircling density of sorrow will weigh on me. Unfortunately, I have learned to compensate for it in moments of ministry, and to most I appear mostly normal. But deep within, an ache of gloom casts an ominous shadow over my soul.

In these moments, delight feels just out of reach. This cloud of darkness is not unbearable in one sense, but the lingering nature of it wearies my spirit. As I wrote to my wife recently about it, "I'm tired of being so frail and unstable. I'm tired of pouting and complaining about it. I'm tired of wallowing in self-pity and inwardly moping again every few months." The combination of my inadequacies and failures within and the problems and pressures without form an abundant concoction of despair.

In the midst of this adversity from the inside, I'm tempted to sin in two specific ways. First, I attempt to "grit and go" by powering through in human strength. Second, I contemplate an escape. Not an escape from life itself, but one from the lot I've been given in pastoral ministry. God is graciously sustaining me. Brothers, some will battle with depression and need the common grace of medicine and medical care. Please do not forsake these potential instruments in the name of spirituality. For many, however, the adversity of spiritual sorrow is something of a recurring moment of realization that all in the world is not right. It leaves us slumping and despondent. If this describes you, do not despair—you're not alone. It won't feel like it in the moment, but even this adversity is a gift.

## ENCOURAGEMENT TO SUFFER WITH TENACITY

Our stories are unique in one sense and ordinary in another. We're not the first or the last to struggle with conflict, crises, illness, and despondency, but our particular trials are deeply personal. Every pastor could write his own chapter, and some could write an entire book. Once again, our heart is neither to trumpet ourselves as exemplary sufferers nor to wallow in self-pity. We have been, by any sensible account, graciously and abundantly blessed. But persevering is never easy. Whether your list is longer or shorter than ours, you will not endure it without the ministry of the Spirit through the word in your life. To this end, consider four encouragements—based once more on Romans 8:28 and 2 Corinthians 1:3–7—to help you suffer with grit and tenacity in your ministry.

**Suffering leads to something good in a pastor's life**

Pastors certainly fall under the category of those who love God and are called according to his purpose. Therefore, all things are working together for our good. Suffering that directly results from the labors of pastoral ministry is no exception as God's providence extends over that as well. In fact, according to the Scripture, suffering that results from following and serving Jesus yields greater blessings.[8] Suffering yields immediately experienced spiritual good as we grow in humility, intimacy with God in prayer, dependence on him, and fuller awareness of his grace. It also yields an eternal spiritual good of preparing us for the glory that awaits us in the end. Press on in and through suffering with full assurance that God is always accomplishing good in you and your ministry.

**Suffering brings the comfort and presence of a loving and merciful God**

Through Paul's reminder to the Corinthians, God encourages believers that he, "the Father of mercies and God of all comfort,"

8 See Matthew 5:11–12, 1 Peter 4:14.

always comforts us. Believers should move toward suffering, embracing it with grit and tenacity, because our merciful God promises to meet us in it and comfort us through it. Not only do we trust in God's word, but we can testify to the sweetness of God's nearness in times of desperation and anguish. Thus, our longing for fellowship with God and the promise of it in suffering equips us to endure suffering.

**Suffering cultivates empathy in caring for hurting people**

The benefits of affliction are not merely personal but extend as they equip us to minister more effectively to others. Empathy, more so than sympathy, allows us to enter into one's suffering by feeling a measure of what they feel. Because the comforter has experienced a hurt like the sufferer's, he can commiserate and encourage with greater awareness and sensitivity. In this way, a pastor's suffering is a gift to him and to the congregation he serves because it prepares him to comfort others in the way God comforted him. Again, Paul makes this connection in writing to the church at Corinth: "so that we may be able to comfort those who are in any affliction, with the comfort with which we ourselves are comforted by God" (2 Cor. 1:4).

**Suffering produces an endurance that brings perseverance**

Prior to the previously mentioned and sweeping promises of Romans 8:28, Paul establishes this truth: "we rejoice in our sufferings, knowing that suffering produces endurance, and endurance produces character, and character produces hope" (Rom. 5:3–4). James also presents this truth clearly in the well-known statement at the beginning of his letter: "Count it all joy, my brothers, when you meet trials of various kinds, for you know that the testing of your faith produces steadfastness." Just as running trains your body to run faster and longer, and weight training makes you stronger, suffering enables you to suffer. The spiritual muscles needed to persevere in pastoral ministry are built and strengthened by and in our trials. Our confidence in the future—hope in God to keep his promises—is forged in the fires of affliction. Therefore, we possess a growing grit and tenacity in suffering because we know it serves us by increasing our strength, durability, and usefulness to the Chief Shepherd.

## PERSONAL REFLECTION

***Brian:*** I don't like to suffer. I fight it constantly. But what I cannot deny is how much God has done not despite my suffering, but in it. So much of my ministry with Practical Shepherding flows out of my story of almost being fired three times, but God redeeming the suffering. So much of the credibility I have with pastors to challenge them to care for themselves and their family comes out of what God taught me through my personal soul despair and my own family implosion. I don't like to suffer, but my most fruitful ministry flows from my suffering. I assume you can say the same thing. Only God can do that in his mysterious and providential plan. I am so thankful I know and serve a God who has the power to achieve this and the mercy to do it this way. His plans have certainly shown themselves to be better than mine.

***James:*** Unfortunately, some lessons must be learned the hard way. I have proved this maxim time and again in my life, and I've seen it displayed in many others. While it would be nice to apply wisdom based on the mistakes and difficulties of others, there is no substitute for personal experience. The past twelve-plus years pastoring the same local church has been an extraordinary grace and privilege. However, it's also been a difficult road. Many of the challenges result from my weaknesses and inadequacies, but the waters have been tumultuous at times. While God has accomplished so much in yielding spiritual fruit and gospel growth, the road has been rough. Looking back, though, I'm thankful for the Lord's kindness in making my way difficult. I am confident that success and ease would have tempted me to pride, self-righteousness, and self-reliance. Instead, his kindness provided trials and suffering to shape me as a man, equip me as a pastor, and fill me with hope.

## CONCLUSION

We conclude this chapter with an oft-used quote from Charles Spurgeon. Pastors, let this become our confession: "I dare say the greatest earthly blessing that God can give to any of us is health, with the exception of sickness. . . . Affliction is the best bit of furniture in my house. It is the best book in a minister's library."[9] May we all embrace this mindset as God's plan for pastors and may it move us to persevere through all we face.

9 Randy Alcorn, If God Is Good: Faith in the Midst of Suffering and Evil (Colorado Springs: Multnomah, 2009), p. 416.

6

# A RESOLVE TO DIE

*For we who live are always being given over to death for Jesus' sake, so that the life of Jesus also may be manifested in our mortal flesh. So death is at work in us, but life in you.*
(2 Cor. 4:11–12)

We are often asked, "Why is pastoral ministry so difficult?" In fact, through our ministry with Practical Shepherding over the past five years, countless men have inquired about the reasons behind the unique nature of the challenges pastors face. A convergence of factors, many related to Covid-19, have created some unique challenges for pastors all over the world more recently. The impact of the Internet and social media have added rare, and perhaps unparalleled, difficulty. While no one can deny the exceptional environment we have experienced recently, both inside and outside the church, the difficulty of pastoral ministry is not unprecedented. Pastors have struggled to persevere in every generation of church history.

The curse of sin causes God to state that work, in every context on earth, will now be filled with toil and striving (Gen. 3:17). Yet, pastoral ministry appears uniquely challenging for a variety of reasons. First, pastors experience more intense spiritual warfare as they work on the frontlines of that battle. The enemy, who fights passionately against any work of God to build his kingdom, seeks to defeat and destroy all his children, but especially those men aspiring to lead.

Second, the pastor's ministry is people-work, and all people are sinners. Of course, believers are saved by God's grace, redeemed by Christ's blood, and indwelt by the Holy Spirit, but all believers are still sinners. To make matters worse, pastors still wrestle with sin themselves. Spiritual warfare, or the ongoing battle against sin and its dominion, permeates every aspect of this work, inwardly and outwardly.

Third, the practical demands of a pastor's job work together to create pressures and expectations on pastors and their families that exceed what most face in ordinary employment. The intensity of this burden is often exacerbated by lower-than-average financial compensation relative to the surrounding community. The challenges of this vocation and life highlight the most quintessential reason a pastor's call is distinctively hard: the call of a pastor is the call to die daily for the sake of the flock.

I (Brian) was first challenged by this idea as I sat with an old friend, an eighty-year-old Scottish pastor, Bill Hughes, who said, "I want to preach until I die, but after forty years of being a pastor, my heart can't take the pastoral work anymore." Coming from one of the most pastorally gifted men I have ever known, these words landed with shock bordering on disbelief. He was so depleted by the rigors of more than four decades of pastoral ministry, nothing could replenish him. No break, vacation, or sabbatical could recover what he had lost. Stunned by his words, they still ring in my ears ten years later. They form the basis for my conviction that the call to die slowly in service to the flock contributes primarily to the uniquely difficult calling of pastoral ministry.

## THE HARDEST WEEK OF MINISTRY

Although I (Brian) could not have articulated it at the time, I felt the weight of this maxim after arguably the hardest week of my ministry. My pastoral mentor and his wife, Jackson and Barbara Boyett, were tragically killed by drunk drivers on a dark Wednesday in November. Two days later, on Friday afternoon, I received word that one of my closest friends in our church, a neighbor and deacon who was my age, had also died in a car accident. His death left a wife and two kids under the age of five to cope with the loss and an uncertain future. The tragedy overwhelmed the members of our close-knit congregation with shock and grief, even while trying to care for this young family. The weight of these losses saddled me with the responsibility of caring not only for this young widow and her kids, but also for a heartbroken church family and for my own devastated family, while, at the same time, trying to deal personally with the grief from these deaths.

As you can imagine, the whirlwind that ensued over the next two weeks was unlike anything I had ever experienced. My heart and mind filled with sadness as I absorbed losing my mentor, his wife, and my friend, while the cloud of sorrow hovered in my home as my wife and children wrestled with it, too. Whenever my attention focused outward, I faced the challenge of serving and helping a devastated congregation that needed to mourn and rally to care for this shattered family. Unavoidably divided by the simultaneous tragedies, I led my friend's funeral in his hometown in Eastern Kentucky while my mentor and his wife were buried in Austin, Texas. This timing prevented me from attending their funeral and from the usual process of facing and working through my own personal grief.

When the dust settled from that hectic couple of weeks, I remember making a surprising and enlightening statement to my wife: "I think something broke and died inside of me this week that is never coming back." These events transpired more than ten years ago, and I stand by that comment even more today. I had suffered a loss in those moments that I couldn't put into words until Bill Hughes' confession to me. Without doubt, pastoral ministry is a call to die. In the cataclysmic events of life, especially those involving the death of a loved one, people suffer a physical, emotional, mental, and spiritual loss akin to death. These overwhelming moments take something from us that is never returned.

In one sense, death does not surprise us as we are all dying in this fallen world. Every day, every person moves closer to this appointment. This reality is unavoidable and unassailable, but we can never properly prepare for the sting of it. Thus, it affects us in life-changing ways. The loss of the closest people in our lives leaves scars that never fully heal this side of eternity. While death provides the clearest glimpse of this effect, it is seen in all of life's calamities. In these various valleys, a piece of each person dies along the way.

## THE JOY IN DYING

As pastors sacrifice themselves to serve Jesus by shepherding his people, we walk through these valleys, over and over again, with our congregation. The frequent and repeated nature of this experience makes pastoral ministry uniquely challenging, especially when this ministry overlaps with our personal crises and valleys. We carry our flock's burdens regularly, but at times the weight is felt similarly or equally by us. The combination of personal and ministry burdens contribute to pastoral burnout, depression, mental and emotional breakdowns, and unexplainable health issues that emerge because of the constant stress. While personal soul care will help pastors endure, the cumulative effect of this suffering—this death of self—is inevitable, and is central to the call of a pastor.

By God's providential kindness, pastors have a privileged, front-row seat to his work in the world. As an under-shepherd of the Chief Shepherd, we have the honor to shepherd the souls of his people, to proclaim the life-giving word of God, to care for God's people in their pain, to sit with elderly saints as they move from this life into eternity, and to invest in this work with everlasting value. We spend our lives in ways that really matter, but it comes at a cost. In this chapter, we will highlight the joyful death that is part of God's plan for every pastor, God's good purposes in it, and why understanding this death is vital for pastoral perseverance.

Paul beautifully articulates the reality of this slow, joyful death as he writes to defend his apostolic ministry to the Corinthians:

> *Therefore, having this ministry by the mercy of God, we do not lose heart. But we have renounced disgraceful, underhanded ways. We refuse to practice cunning or to tamper with God's word, but by the open statement of the truth we would commend ourselves to everyone's conscience in the sight of God. And even if our gospel is veiled, it is veiled to those who are perishing. In their case the god of this world has blinded the minds of the unbelievers, to keep them from seeing the light of the gospel of the glory of Christ, who is the image of God. For what we proclaim is not ourselves, but Jesus Christ as Lord, with ourselves as your servants for Jesus' sake. For God, who said, "Let light shine out of darkness," has shone in our hearts to give the light of the knowledge of the glory of God in the face of Jesus Christ.*
>
> *But we have this treasure in jars of clay, to show that the surpassing power belongs to God and not to us. We are afflicted in every way, but not crushed; perplexed, but not driven to*

> *despair; persecuted, but not forsaken; struck down, but not destroyed; always carrying in the body the death of Jesus, so that the life of Jesus may also be manifested in our bodies. For we who live are always being given over to death for Jesus' sake, so that the life of Jesus also may be manifested in our mortal flesh. So death is at work in us, but life in you.*
>
> *Since we have the same spirit of faith according to what has been written, "I believed, and so I spoke," we also believe, and so we also speak, knowing that he who raised the Lord Jesus will raise us also with Jesus and bring us with you into his presence. For it is all for your sake, so that as grace extends to more and more people it may increase thanksgiving, to the glory of God.*
>
> *So we do not lose heart. Though our outer self is wasting away, our inner self is being renewed day by day. For this light momentary affliction is preparing for us an eternal weight of glory beyond all comparison, as we look not to the things that are seen but to the things that are unseen. For the things that are seen are transient, but the things that are unseen are eternal (2 Cor. 4:1–18).*

This type of slow dying naturally leads to human despair. But empowered by God and stabilized by his perspective, Paul bookends his description of ministry with these words: "we do not lose heart" (2 Cor. 4:1 and 16). The demands of our calling leave us physically, mentally, emotionally, and at times even spiritually depleted. Spent, drained, and pushed beyond our human breaking point, we are not forsaken, ruined, or destroyed. In fact, God uses this dying to bring a unique joy to the pastor. Paul provides four reasons pastors experience joy in the midst of pastoral death.

**We are joyful because suffering reminds us that we carry eternal treasure in our frail bodies**

A pastor and his ministry are, by nature, unimpressive vessels carrying the most precious treasure. The treasure is the gospel (v. 3), or "the light of the knowledge of the glory of God in the face of Jesus Christ" (v. 6). We, the container, are "jars of clay," or a weakened and frail human body, which houses this prize to show that the "power belongs to God and not to us" (v. 7). Our faltering bodies do not surprise or alarm us because we know what they are and what they are used by God to do. By his gracious plan, the strength to persevere comes not from our human ability, but from the One who has placed this treasure in us. This truth eliminates all pride for pastors and releases them from the misguided pressure of impressing others.

**We are joyful because our dying brings life to the flock**

The pastor's death to himself in his ministry bears an unexpected result: life in others. Paul describes his dying with vivid, memorable terms. In verses 8–9 he offers four couplets where, in each case, the former represents what he has faced, while the latter clarifies that in no case has the suffering reached its worst degree. He has been afflicted, perplexed, persecuted, and struck down, but he has never been crushed, despairing, forsaken, or destroyed. As with all followers of Jesus, he was sharing in Christ's sufferings so that Christ's life would be manifested in him. This principle—dying to self for Christ results in abundant life—echoes throughout the New Testament and is stated straightforwardly here: "We who live are always being given over to death for Jesus' sake, so that the life of Jesus also may be manifested in our mortal flesh" (v. 11). Then in reference to his ministry, Paul declares, "So death is at work in us, but life in you" (v. 12).

God brings life in his people through the death of his pastors. These sobering words make perfect sense. Jesus laid down his life for his sheep, and in a similar way, he calls under-shepherds to lay down their lives for the flock under their care. Of course, Jesus' death bears substitutionary significance for each of his followers in ways that we cannot parallel, but our suffering is an instrument for cultivating spiritual progress, or life, in them. Can you imagine a more meaningful way to live as a follower of Jesus than to die for the spiritual good of Christ's people?

**We are joyful because Jesus will raise us to eternal life in the end**

We gladly lay down our lives for others because of our confidence in God's ultimate promise to us. We can endure suffering on behalf of and even at the hands of difficult, wayward, and divisive sheep because the glory that awaits will far exceed the suffering (v. 17). All the death experienced in this world will one day be swallowed up by life when Jesus raises us and brings us into his presence (v. 14). Therefore, pastors are strengthened to endure by the promise of eternal life.

**We are joyful because the inner self is being renewed as we die**

The blessings received through this death are not confined to the distant future. Rather, we enjoy immediate gain through our suffering. Even as his outer self wastes away, the pastor's inner self is renewed daily. Paul reiterated this truth in Romans 5:3–4 when he wrote that sufferings produce endurance, which yields character, which leads to hope. While he doesn't use the word hope in 2 Corinthians as he does in Romans, the concept is clearly central. Temporary affliction produces eternal good because it stirs hope in us and prepares for us an eternal glory that is incomparably greater (2 Cor. 4:16–18). Therefore, pastors joyfully lay down their lives for others because our perspective is shaped by eternity, knowing it cultivates spiritual good in others and in us, and it culminates in an everlasting reward.

## A PRICE WORTH PAYING

This call to come and die for Christ is not the type of invitation that ordinarily generates a positive response. Even though Paul provides compelling reasons for pastors to embrace this death, his description surely fails as a recruitment tool. Few sober-minded men would sign up for the emotional and spiritual job hazards combined with the financial and family risks, much less the promise of death on behalf of others. But while many opt for the apparent security of secular employment, the potential for more money, and the American dream of comfortable living, God has supplied men for this labor in every generation. The men who answer this call do so because they believe, like tens of thousands before them, that pastoral ministry is worth the price it exacts from them. The following descriptions give reasons for enlisting in this work and provide stability for pastors to stay, endure, and even thrive in their respective places of ministry.

### Pastoral ministry is a joyful call

This unique death brings unique joy. In our (Brian and James) combined ministry of more than fifty years, the joys we've known are too numerous to list. We have been privileged to lead God's people by feeding them with God's word. Likewise, we have offered warnings and encouragement from his word to straying and wandering souls. We have joined in key moments of their lives by officiating at weddings, celebrating anniversaries, and welcoming new children. We have watched the Spirit work to give new birth to previously hard and dead hearts. We have seen believers grow in strength, devotion, purity, and love through tender admonition. We have experienced the church at her best in caring for one another during the moments of deepest grief and suffering. We have walked the final steps with people as they entered eternity and proclaimed hope through the gospel at the funerals which followed. The pastor's work offers the unique joy of shepherding the souls of God's people, and this joy cultivates perseverance.

**Pastoral ministry is a meaningful call**

While it is not the only important vocation in the world, the value of pastoral ministry exceeds all others. We minister with words of life that cross into eternity, helping people navigate their earthly pilgrimage with an eye toward ultimate reality. Our work intersects with the ordinary affairs of life to infuse them with supernatural concerns that will outlast them. As people wrestle with meaning and significance in the monotony of daily life, for example, we offer hope and help that supersedes it all. Amid the earthly labors that provide assistance in the present and can even leave a lasting mark on culture and society, our task is greater because the results are not confined to this present world. Instead, our work counts for eternity. This eternal perspective frames the pastor's work and helps him press through trials and discouragement.

**Pastoral ministry is a privileged call**

God gives each of us only one life, and to pastors he gives the honor of spending it as his appointed under-shepherds. We get to serve the same sheep for whom Jesus laid down his life and whom he purchased by his blood. The basic thrust of the tender and weighty commission given to Peter in John 21 extends to pastors, who now feed and tend to this flock. Even though wounded, frightened, and suffering sheep may bite and resist us, pastors bear the unique responsibility to guide, care, and even protect them from danger under God's authority. Pastors step between them and the wolves, who are armed and sent by the enemy to destroy and devour them. We live in the privileged place of continuing the earthly ministry of Jesus and caring for his sheep. Although the costs are great, the honor of serving our King by tending to his flock is greater.

## PEACE IN DYING

This joyful yet grueling labor takes a toll on the man who fulfills it. The pastor who lives in perpetual death for the sake of others pays a price in his soul, especially the man who endures over the long term. What should he expect to be the state of his soul after a full life lived dying for the sake of his flock? Once again, my (Brian) mentor and friend Bill Hughes planted the seed of this answer more than a decade ago: "After a lifetime of ministry, the faithful pastor finishes with a peaceful, broken heart."

This statement swells with profound wisdom and insight. Lifelong pastoral ministry, fulfilled rightly, yields a peaceful heart devoid of bitterness and resentment. Despite the scars from years of conflict, affliction, and betrayal, and the battle-weariness, the pastor can rest in quiet contentment that only God provides by his Spirit. While no one discharges his responsibilities perfectly, God gives assurance and peace to men who strive to honor him with their lives and ministries. Despite the temptations to shrink back, harden, close off, and grow cynical, the man who turns to God for refuge is renewed. While still tender, the scars of ministry leave a lasting imprint of brokenness. Although the dying to self in ministry ushers in pain, sorrow, and heartache that irreversibly affect the heart, the man finishes his race at peace with God and his ministry.

This description captures beautifully the center of a man who spends his life in faithful service to his Master and concludes that service without regret.

We suspect (and hope) many readers are pastors enduring in pastoral ministry. Perhaps your experience matches Paul's depiction of pastoral death in 2 Corinthians 4, and you wonder how you will persevere without losing heart. We will recommend three activities for soul care to help you pursue a "peaceful, but broken heart."

**Embrace weakness**

This death associated with gospel ministry is a fundamental part of God's plan. Rather than kicking against it or trying to avoid it, pastors must embrace it and the weakness it exposes. In fact, the reminder of our human frailty provides the platform for the manifestation of Christ's power in us. Paul articulates this concept more fully in chapter 12 of 2 Corinthians. Through suffering and trials, God taught him to embrace weaknesses so that he would know the power of Christ and come even to boast in his weakness (2 Cor. 12:9–10). The echoes of his reference to the treasure hidden in jars of clay (4:7) are unmistakable.

Pastors are well-acquainted with weakness. We minister with limited capacities, physical frailties, mental and emotional struggles, and spiritual battles with sin. We can claim no sovereignty over circumstance or conquest over sin. We are humans who must embrace our humanity as clay jars while knowing that we carry an inestimable treasure. This is our means of persevering.

One key component of embracing weakness is refusing to live by comparison with other pastors. While weakness is universal, the experience of it is relative based on each man's God-given composition, gifting, and circumstances. In other words, pastors experience this death differently and at varied rates. I (Brian) still deal with the lingering effects of physical issues and family trials from my first five years in a challenging field of pastoral ministry. Because some pastors are blessed with higher thresholds for enduring under suffering, personal attacks, grief, and pain, all must live with the awareness of how God has made us and embrace who we are—weaknesses and all. Living in this reality will help a pastor persevere.

**Engage grief**

Because death plays a large part of a pastor's life, he must face grief head-on. This includes acknowledging the pain of losing church members and friends to death, even though he often pushes his emotions aside in ministering to the families. In addition, pastors must regularly recognize the sorrow associated with suffering, loss of relationships, personal attacks, criticism, and betrayal. A refusal to confront grief often leads to bitterness. Therefore, we must engage the sadness with a willingness to express it and receive comfort from others. This process promotes healing in the soul and yields compassion and empathy.

I (Brian) must confess that for a long time I avoided feelings of sadness in my life. Thankfully, a friend confronted me. When I challenged him to give me a good reason to embrace sadness, his reply surprised me: "You need to embrace sadness in your life because Jesus was a man of sorrows acquainted with grief." God used those words as a catalyst. I have since come to realize that sadness and grief are healing for the soul. As I learned to embrace the grief of pastoral ministry, I began facing the death of pastoral ministry with hope. This hope is critical for persevering and not losing heart.

**Experience joy**

Pastors who live much of their lives in the throes of death often struggle to appreciate and celebrate the joys of ministry. Afraid and anxious about the next battle or ministry struggle, they miss the gladness from what God is accomplishing all around them. While we must not whistle lightheartedly when the moment calls for gravity, pastors must maintain and demonstrate an effervescent, soul-level delight. Despite the suffering and loss that so often surrounds us, we have permission to feel joy. Moreover, this joy fosters perseverance. Pastors must look for spiritual fruit and the evidence of God's grace in themselves to help spur them on in their labors.

Joy and sadness are often pitted against each other, but they enjoy a beautiful, interdependent relationship. The co-existence of joy and sadness—experienced throughout this ministry of death—cultivates a peaceful, broken heart in the soul of a pastor. Ultimately, our joy comes from knowing Christ, but the added joy of ministry supplements our hearts in times of sorrow. When pastors allow themselves the freedom to enjoy this labor, it becomes an instrument of perseverance to help them thrive in their place of ministry.

## PERSONAL REFLECTION

***Brian:*** This chapter has been a labor of love five years in the making. As we work with a few thousand pastors every year at Practical Shepherding, we get asked this difficult question regularly. Paul's teaching and this concept of a unique pastoral death has become a helpful way to explain what so many pastors are enduring after many years of ministry. After ten to twenty years of pastoral ministry, pastors start to have mysterious physical issues rise to the surface, weird bouts with brain fog, and a strange emotional and spiritual fatigue that doctors find puzzling. I have personally experienced many of these realities, which tangibly improved with rest and personal soul care. Certainly, there are many possible causes to these symptoms, but the death pastors experience in this eternal work is a realistic explanation for the unexplainable aspects in their lives.

***James:*** Like Brian, I struggle to acknowledge and process the emotions that come with pastoral ministry. My natural disposition is more logical and analytical, so it seems easier to suppress sadness and to power through in ministering to others. This approach, however, is neither wise nor tenable. While it may feel like strength in the moment, the refusal to embrace these feelings is weakness. And even though it seems the weight lifts when the trying situation passes, the cumulative burden builds. God has been gracious to use friendships to press me when I'm tempted to ignore the personal weight of ministry and to encourage me along the way.[1]

## CONCLUSION

Until pastors embrace weakness, engage grief, and experience joy in the face of this pastoral death, they will not find the stamina to press on, endure, and thrive in this work. This call to die daily for the sake of our flock is a noble and eternally significant one because it yields life in them. While exacting a great price from us, it brings an inexpressible joy. So, brothers, let us die well knowing with confidence that Jesus will be with us to the end. He will sustain you. He will keep you. He will carry you to the end.

1 See Pastoral Friendship.

# CONCLUSION

Only God knows of the countless men who have labored in difficult fields over the centuries, but few recorded stories match the hostility Charles Simeon endured at the hands of his own congregation. Their relationship began poorly and only descended from there. Despite vocal opposition from the church, the bishop appointed Simeon as minister of Holy Trinity Church in Cambridge in November 1782. In the months leading to this appointment, the parishioners not only opposed him, but petitioned the bishop to have their curate, John Hammond, installed as minister. Hammond had served them in this role for some time and they made their preference for him clearly known.

When the petition was denied, the parishioners turned to political maneuvering in an attempt to manipulate the bishop. At that time, the primary income source for a minister came from the lectureship in the church. While the lecturer was almost always the minister, the congregation held the authority to select that person separate from the bishop's appointment. Knowing of the bishop's intent to appoint Simeon, the congregation threatened to give the lectureship, and thus the primary source of income, to Hammond no matter who was appointed as their minister.

Aware of the brewing controversy, Simeon expressed to the congregation his desire for peace and willingness to step aside, and considered writing likewise to the bishop. Ultimately, he decided to await the bishop's response to the church's petition and accept his decision. The bishop was undeterred by the church's threat and offered the position to Simeon. In addition, he made clear to Simeon that regardless of whether he accepted the post, Hammond would not receive it.

All parties followed through on their promises. Bishop Yorke appointed Simeon. Simeon accepted the position. The congregation appointed Hammond as lecturer. Hammond taught every Sunday afternoon and received income from it. Derek Prime captures the setting well: "Scarcely a worse start to a ministry could be imagined. The sense of hostility was tangible. His pastoral wish to visit people was impossible because of their bitterness at his appointment: none would admit him to their homes."[1]

The intensity of the hostility was matched only by its longevity. Biographer Handley Moule remarks, "Long and painful was the siege laid against Simeon's activity and influence."[2] He assumed his responsibility to preach on Sunday mornings, but the parishioners stood in his way. They refused to attend and even locked their pews so no one could use their seats. Simeon responded by bringing in benches and seats at his own expense, only to have them thrown out by the churchwardens. After several months, he began Sunday evening lectures from the Scripture, but again the churchwardens tried to prevent him. They shut the doors on him, and on one occasion even locked the doors and left with the key. This opposition lasted more than a decade. Hammond continued as lecturer for five years before the job was then given to a parishioner's son, once more instead of Simeon. He would not assume that responsibility until 1794, twelve years after his appointment as minister.

1 Derek Prime, *Charles Simeon: An Ordinary Pastor of Extraordinary Influence*. (Leominster: Day One, 2011), p. 46.

2 Handley Moule, *Charles Simeon: Pastor of a Generation* (Fearn, Ross-shire: Christian Focus, 1997), p. 42.

What was Simeon's response to this open hostility? He did not strike back. He patiently, persistently preached and shepherded souls. After coming to check on him, his mentor, Henry Venn, wrote, "He preaches twice a week . . . and his people are indeed of an excellent spirit—merciful, loving, and righteous."[3] He ascended the pulpit every Sunday morning to exposit God's word. He spent much of his weekly grind shepherding the souls of his flock. And in an extremely rare move, he held a Sunday evening lecture in a large room in another church's parish. Even more, Simeon committed himself to the Lord, trusting in him without angst or bitterness.

For more than fifty years, Simeon faithfully preached and shepherded the souls of that one congregation. The essence of his ministry shines through his twenty-one-volume work, *Horae Homileticae*, that contains chapter-by-chapter commentary and sermon outlines on every book of the Bible. Simeon's words about God's purposes and plans for him as a follower of Jesus and a pastor are as remarkable as they are powerful:

> *[God] knew the real desire of my heart; he knew that I only wished to fulfil his will. I told him a thousand times over that I did not deprecate persecution; for I considered that as the necessary lot of all who would "live godly in Christ Jesus"; and more especially, of all who would preach Christ with fidelity.*[4]

These beautiful words capture well a proper understanding of God's call upon a pastor. As this book has sought to articulate, this call is not unique to Simeon or to his era of church history. Rather, the call to persevere is one rooted in the promises of God

---

3 Prime, *Charles Simeon*, p. 47.

4 Prime, *Charles Simeon*, p. 47.

and extends through the exhortations of Scripture. Regardless of the context, time, country, or culture, pastors must embrace God's plan to qualify, take heed, shepherd, preach, suffer, and die. These six actions provide a framework of faithfulness for all pastors.

The goal, however, is not mere faithfulness, but a joyful contentment in Christ and an eager gladness for this work. When governed by God's word and empowered by his Spirit, the pastor finds the strength and ability to hold fast, to stay where God has planted him, to endure through the suffering and difficulties, and ultimately to persevere until God releases him from the work in that place.

www.epbooks.org

EP Books, also called **Evangelical Press**,
is a long-established UK publisher of
**Christian book**s that exists to serve the church,
and a division of **10ofthose.com**